A Companion

for

Daniel Kolak's

Lovers of Wisdom
A Historical Introduction to Philosophy
with Integrated Readings

Second Edition

D1561075

Joe Salerno
William Paterson University

WADSWORTH

THOMSON LEARNING ™

Australia • Canada • Mexico • Singapore • Spain • United Kingdom • United States

For more information, contact
Wadsworth/Thomson Learning
10 Davis Drive
Belmont, CA 94002-3098
USA

For more information about our products, contact us:
Thomson Learning Academic Resource Center
1-800-423-0563
http://www.wadsworth.com

International Headquarters
Thomson Learning
International Division
290 Harbor Drive, 2nd Floor
Stamford, CT 06902-7477
USA

UK/Europe/Middle East/South Africa
Thomson Learning
Berkshire House
168-173 High Holborn
London WC1V 7AA
United Kingdom

Asia
Thomson Learning
60 Albert Complex, #15-01
Singapore 189969

Canada
Nelson Thomson Learning
1120 Birchmount Road
Toronto, Ontario M1K 5G4
Canada

CONTENTS

PREFACE

Based on the original edition by Joe Salerno, Hope May, and Michael Russo, the second edition of the *Companion for Kolak's Lovers of Wisdom* is a guide to the activity of philosophy. It is a guide for open-minded students in their quest for ideas, insights and answers to great philosophical questions. The mission of this text is to facilitate understanding of several philosophical insights by engaging the student in the very methods of the philosophers being studied. For it is one thing to be told what the philosophers said, and quite another thing to participate in their philosophical investigations: to perform their thought-experiments, to have one's own meditations, and to analyze and evaluate the logic oneself. One should emerge with an increased ability to do one's own creative and original philosophy.

For each chapter in *Lovers of Wisdom* there is a corresponding chapter herein, which includes supplemental instruction, writing assignments, thought-experiments and/or activities for further contemplation of the material.

Chapter 1

The First Philosophers

Thales, Anaximander, Anaximenes

What is the Nature of Reality?

Thales claimed that "everything is water." Anaximander thought that "everything is the infinite boundless." And Anaximenes said that "everything is air." Is it possible that they really believed these claims? Certainly. We could stop here and just laugh at their underdeveloped, bottom-of-the-barrel metaphysics. Or we could be philosophers. We could try to understand *what* it is that they were saying and *why* they said it. More simply we could attempt to understand why *anyone* would put forth such claims at all. All this is to say that we could -- as contemporary philosophers -- make an effort to understand the Milesian philosophers.

The philosophical question is this:

What is the underlying nature of reality?

That was the question asked by the Milesian philosophers. They wanted to know what the entire world ultimately consists in. What is this stuff around us? Yes, yes, books, and tables, and earth, but what is all that stuff made of? What is the most basic constituent of reality? Now to really understand the Milesian answers, one must make turn the question into one about the reality in which you live. Only then, will we be in a better position to do our own creative and original philosophy? Let's prepare.

In claiming that everything reduces to a single kind of stuff, each of the Milesians is tacitly claiming that human perceptions misrepresent reality. They are claiming that our familiar perceptions misrepresent the true nature of things. Appearance and reality pull apart!

Exercise

1.   Do you agree with the Milesians' tacit claim that human perceptions misrepresent reality? Or do you believe that ordinary human perceptions reveal the true nature of reality? Ask yourself what *you* take everything to be made of (it does not necessarily have to be just one thing). Take your time, and after you have given it some thought, record your answer.

Everything is made of...

Does your answer refer to something perceivable? If you answered that everything is made of "atoms" or "quarks," then you do not believe that ordinary human perceptions offer a accurate picture of reality. After all, neither atoms nor quarks are familiar objects of experience. In fact, it is generally agreed that they are not even *possible* objects of experience; they are called "unobservables." But perhaps you gave an answer which is more rooted in experience than are "atoms" and "quarks." For instance, perhaps you said that everything is made of light. Nonetheless, if your theory reduces everything to a single kind of stuff (say, water, air or light), or even a very few kinds of stuff (say, the elements of the periodic table), then your theory implies that appearances fall far short of reality. For, our everyday perceptions do not reveal that everything is made of something more basic.

How Can We Describe Reality?

If it is true that appearance and reality radically pull apart, then the problem arises as to how we should proceed in describing the nature of reality. Should we describe reality with concepts that are, to the highest degree possible, unrelated to human experience? If we choose to describe reality with terms that do *not* refer to objects of our experience, we are faced with the question of how we can know what we are talking about. There is also the problem of how we can know whether what we are saying is true. After all, it seems that you cannot verify that which is beyond all human experience. On the other hand, if we choose to describe reality with terms that *are* rooted in human experience, then we are faced with the problem of how we can have knowledge of the world as it is *independently* of human experience.

THEORETICIAN'S DILEMMA	
Does the Theory Of Reality Make Use Of Terms Rooted In Human Experience?	**Problem**
Yes	How can we gain knowledge of the reality that transcends human experience?
No	How can we know whether our theory refers to anything that is "out there?" How can we know that our theory is true?

Exercise

2.   Consider your view concerning the relationship between perception and reality. Do you think that reality can be understood by means of completely abstract concepts, as Anaximander attempted to do, or, do you think, like Thales and Anaximenes, that we must describe reality with concepts that are rooted in human experience? Indicate this below by circling the appropriate word:

Reality can/ cannot be described with concepts that refer to human perceptions.

If you indicated that reality *can* be described with concepts referring to human perceptions, but, in completing exercise 1 above, you indicated that everything is made of, say, atoms, then you appear to be contradicting yourself, and your view is therefore problematic. In this case, you say that reality should be described with concepts which refer to elements of human perceptions, but you describe reality in terms of a concept which does *not* refer to anything perceivable; namely, the concept of atoms. So, you say something about reality in exercise 1, and then you say that those sorts of things cannot be said in exercise 2. Similarly, your view will also be problematic if you believe that reality can*not* be described with concepts referring to humanly perceivable things, while at the same time you believe (in exercise 1) that everything is made of something which *is* perceptually familiar.

Exercise

3.   Determine whether your answers to exercise 1 and 2 are consistent. That is, make sure that in completing 1 you do not do what you say cannot be done in 2. If you realize that your view is inconsistent, modify it in a way which eliminates this tension.

Everything is made of ...

Reality can/cannot be described with concepts which refer to human perceptions.

The Milesians avoided the inconsistencies we have just mentioned. But, their views certainly had other problems. By both becoming aware of theoretical limitations and replacing faulty theories with ones that are less faulty, we converge on the truth.

Rational Criticism

We will call the two-step process of becoming aware of the limitations of a theory and replacing that theory with one that is less problematic the process of *rational criticism*.

(i) The limitations of a given theory are made explicit by revealing an inherent shortcoming or by providing a counterexample to the theory.

(ii) The given theory is modified to overcome the limitations revealed in (i).

This process, which is integral to the practice of democracy, science, and philosophy, was originated in the West by the Milesians, and has remained one of the most important practices of the Western World ever since. Why is rational criticism important? *At least* for this reason. In revealing theoretical shortcomings, we are motivated to construct alternative theories that are more accurate. And as we construct these alternative theories, we are brought closer to the truth. Because it can bring us closer to the truth, rational criticism is one of our most powerful ways of learning about the world and about ourselves.

How did the Milesians engage in rational criticism? Anaximander realized why Thales' theory was wrong, and he accordingly offered a better one in its place. Anaximenes, who thought that Anaximander was mistaken, articulated what he took to be the better view. Here is a summary of the intellectual evolution of Milesian philosophy that was motivated by rational criticism:

THALES: Everything is water.

ANAXIMANDER: No. Fire exists, and if everything was water, fire could never be. Everything is the infinite boundless!

ANAXIMENES: You are right, Anaximander, in thinking that everything cannot be water, but your theory of reality is unintelligible! Everything is air.

Dialogue and debate are integral parts of rational criticism. Try to persuade someone in your class who has a different theory, with *reasons*, that your theory is better. If someone points out a real difficulty in your theory, one that you cannot resolve, you should thank them! For their observation helps you to see where the flaw is, and it helps you realize that you perhaps knew less than you thought you knew -- you become Socratically wise. Furthermore, in fixing your theory, you walk away with a better theory.

Exercise
4.   Even if you have changed your theory because someone else found a problem with it, try to construct *your own* refutation in the form of a dialogue similar to the conversation sketched above between Thales, Anaximander, and Anaximenes.

My view of the nature of reality is

The problem with this view is

A less problematic view is

The above exercises are valuable, not only because they help you to make explicit to yourself what you believe, but because they also help you to *learn from your mistakes.* In doing so, you engage in an invaluable activity originated by the Milesians. You engage in philosophy.

Pythagoras

Everything is Number

At first glance, the Pythagorean claim that "everything is made of numbers" is just as strange as Thales' claim that everything is made of water. At second glance, however, Pythagoras' claim is even stranger. For, even though Thales' claim does not seem true, it is at least imaginable -- we can imagine that, just as water turns into ice when it freezes, water turns into rocks and trees and everything else under the right conditions. In this case we are imagining that everything with which we are familiar (for instance, wood, air, metal, etc.) is made out of some basic material (namely, water) that is also familiar to us. But how are we to imagine the truth of Pythagoras' claim? How are we to understand that the different materials with which we are familiar are "made out of" non-material things -- namely, numbers? Unlike tiny molecules of water, numbers are not objects in space or time. How, then, can the things in space and time be "made out of" numbers?

At third glance, however, Pythagoras' claim is not all that crazy. If we believe, for instance, that we can understand Reality through physics, then there is a sense in which we endorse Pythagoras' claim. For within physics, nature and its properties are understood *mathematically.* Acceleration, for example, is understood as the change in distance divided by the change in time. Thus, a common phenomenon (acceleration) is understood to consist in a relationship between quantities that are given numerical representations (in terms of distance and time). Moreover, according to modern chemistry, the difference between, say, oxygen and gold, amounts to a difference between their respective "mathematical properties." Modern chemistry describes both oxygen and gold as being made out of the same kinds of "materials": electrons, protons, and neutrons. But oxygen is different than gold since an atom of oxygen has 8 electrons, 8 protons, and 7.9994 neutrons, while an atom of gold has 79 electrons, 79 protons, and 117.967 neutrons. In terms of what oxygen and gold are *made out of,* that is the only difference. Thus both physics and chemistry appear to endorse Pythagoras' claim in some sense. For within both of these disciplines, processes (say, acceleration) and elements (say, oxygen and gold) are understood in terms of relationships between numerical quantities.

Pythagoras, of course, knew neither modern physics nor modern chemistry. Nonetheless, he did believe, as Aristotle puts it, that "the principles of mathematics are the principles of all things...[and] the elements of numbers are the elements of everything." So, we introduced the examples above to imagine a sense in which Pythagoras' claim not only *could be* true, but, according to certain scientific disciplines, *is* true. But maybe Pythagoras meant something deeper. We have merely brought out *one* way of understanding the claim that "everything is made of numbers." Although we do not quite capture the whole of Pythagoras' mystical view, we have given examples that suggest that numerical and mathematical *properties* are at root the underlying structure and essence of everything.

Irrational Magnitudes

The discovery of irrational magnitudes initially shocked the Pythagoreans so badly, that they drowned the Pythagorean who discovered them.[1] Why was this discovery so

---

[1]The story is told by Proclus. See Carl Boyer, *The History of the Calculus and its Conceptual Development* Dover. 1949.

4

moving? Pythagoras, as you know, believed that numbers were the basis of everything. But, initially, he also believed that all numbers are *rational* numbers, the kind of numbers that can be expressed by integers (whole numbers such as 2, 3, 4, etc.) or by the quotient of two integers (fractions such as 6/2, 1/2, 7/8, etc.). The view that everything is number and that all numbers are rational numbers was part of the Pythagoreans' understanding of the world as a harmonious, ordered, and ultimately knowable and beautiful creation. The discovery of *ir*rational magnitudes, however, revealed a problem with this world-view. For irrational magnitudes can be expressed neither as integers, nor as the quotients of integers. These magnitudes can therefore only be represented by "irrational numbers." Pi (π = 3.14159...), which denotes the ratio of the circumference of a circle to its diameter, and $\sqrt{2}$ are well known examples of irrational numbers.

Rational Criticism and Three Reactions to Irrational Magnitudes

The discovery of irrational magnitudes also further illustrates the importance of rational criticism. We can show this by considering the three ways that Pythagoreans reacted to the discovery of irrationals.[2] You now know that there were three groups of Pythagoreans: the "mystical," the "rational," and the "philosophical," each group reacting differently to the discovery. Only one of these groups, however, responded to irrational magnitudes in a way that clearly exemplifies rational criticism.

In order to better understand how the responses of the three groups differ, first ask yourself how is it that *you* react when someone points out that you are mistaken about something. If you get frustrated and say something like, "oh, it doesn't matter, nobody can know the answer anyway,"? you react as the mystical followers of Pythagoras did. Upon realizing that their theory was problematic, the mystics concluded that this shows that humans are not equipped to understand Reality. They "gave up" in the face of criticism, and in doing so were certainly not involved in the activity of rational criticism. Rational criticism, remember, is a two-step process: first, revealing the limitations of a theory, and second, replacing the old theory with a new one that is free of those limitations. Although the mystics admitted that there were problems with Pythagoras' view, they clearly avoided the second step of rational criticism. The mystics, in other words, did not try to solve the problem of irrational magnitudes, but instead, *withdrew from inquiry*.

Perhaps you do not react to criticism in the way described above. Instead, when criticized, when shown that your theory is mistaken, you might "stick to your guns" and convince yourself that any problems that others see in your theory are not very serious. This is how the rational followers of Pythagoras reacted to the discovery of irrational magnitudes. When these thinkers realized that Pythagoras' theory was problematic, they responded by "squeezing" the irrational magnitudes into rational ones. In other words, they treated the irrational magnitudes *as if* they were rational ones. In reacting this way, the rational Pythagoreans failed to engage themselves in rational criticism. For the rational Pythagoreans not only refused to admit to themselves that a real problem existed, but they also avoided replacing Pythagoras' problematic theory with one that was less problematic.

There is another way by which one can react to the criticism of a theory -- the way in which the philosophically minded Pythagoreans reacted. If in the face of criticism you try to strengthen your theory by making the appropriate modifications, you react as the philosophically minded philosophers reacted to the discovery of irrational magnitudes. Upon realizing that the existence of irrational magnitudes could be proved, this group of Pythagoreans admitted that there was more to Reality than rational numbers. The philosophically minded Pythagoreans realized that their original understanding of numbers was incomplete, that their mentor's theory was mistaken, and they began to treat irrational magnitudes as *other kinds of numbers*. The philosophically minded Pythagoreans, in other words, changed their theory in a way that accounted for the existence of irrational

---

[2]See more on the connections between rational criticism and the discovery of irrational magnitudes at the end of Chapter 8.

magnitudes.   In doing so, the philosophically minded Pythagoreans deepened their understanding of the concept of number.

Rational criticism is a two-step method that promotes the advancement of one's understanding of something (say, the nature of wisdom, Reality, the concept of number). Although each of the three groups of Pythagoreans engaged in the first step of rational criticism, only the philosophically minded Pythagoreans engaged in the second.

Exercise

1.   Why do you think that both the mystical and rational followers of Pythagoras failed to advance their understanding of the nature of number? Why does anyone react to criticism in these two ways?

Heraclitus, Parmenides, Zeno of Elea, Democritus

The Dynamicists and the Staticists

What were "the dynamicists" and "the staticists" arguing about? Heraclitus and Democritus were dynamicists. Parmenides and Zeno were staticists. The dynamicists believed that our perception of change and motion corresponds to a feature of Reality, and denied that staticity is real. The staticists maintained that our perception of staticity corresponds to a feature of Reality, and denied that change and motion are real. The debate between the two raises some fundamental philosophical questions:

> (i) what is our most trustworthy source of knowledge; (mathematical) reason or perception?, and

> (ii) what kinds of concepts should be used to describe reality; concepts referring to appearances and perceptions or appearance-transcendent concepts?[3]

Let's examine this debate in terms of these questions.

Zeno's paradox of motion makes live the question of whether mathematical knowledge is more reliable than perceptual knowledge. The dynamicists formulated their theories in accord with perception, and hence in accord with perceptual knowledge. They saw that things were in motion and argued, among other things, that motion is real. Indeed, since we are constantly perceiving things that are in motion, it is understandable why the dynamicists' made this claim. But despite the plausibility of theories that affirm the reality of motion, Zeno argued that any such theory is mistaken. Zeno, as we shall see, formulated his theory not in accord with perception, but in accord with mathematics.

Exercise

1.   Based on what you read in §1.7 of *Lovers of Wisdom*, how does Zeno argue that the possibility of motion contradicts mathematics?

Let's look more closely at Zeno's paradox. Note that, since he concludes from his paradox that motion is illusory, Zeno implicitly assumes that the *mathematical* concept of "distance" corresponds to Reality. In other words, Zeno believed that because the mathematical representation of distance precluded the possibility of motion, motion must therefore be impossible. According to Zeno, Reality *must*   agree with the results of

---

[3]We have already considered this question in connection with the Milesians. For instance, although Anaximander and Anaximenes both endorsed the claim that eyes are not windows, they disagreed about whether we should use concepts which refer to human perceptions in the description of Reality. Anaximander, you will recall, claimed that since eyes are not windows, Reality should not be described with concepts that refer to things we perceive (like water or air), while Anaximenes claimed the opposite.

mathematics. So, Zeno, much like Pythagoras, believed that Reality conforms to the results of mathematics, and thus that it is our most trustworthy source of knowledge.

But does Zeno's argument *prove* that motion is illusory, and thus refute the dynamicists? The dynamicist has two ways to respond to Zeno: (i) deny that there really is a contradiction between the mathematical concept of distance and the perceptual awareness of motion, or (ii) accept that there is a contradiction, and argue that the perceptual side should win out. A dynamicist taking option (ii) could respond to Zeno by arguing that the conclusion that he draws from his paradox is mistaken. For, she might argue, Zeno's paradox does not show that motion is impossible, but rather it shows that the mathematical concept of "distance" is mistaken. Because our perceptual awareness precludes the possibility of things *not* being in motion, mathematics is wrong. In other words, this dynamicist might argue that since motion clearly is possible, it is impossible for there to be an infinite number of points between any two places!

It is not clear what to do. To side with Zeno and the staticists is to deny that motion is real and to implicitly affirm that mathematical knowledge is superior to perceptual knowledge. On the other hand, siding with the dynamicists entails both denying that there is an infinity of points between any two places, and affirming that perceptual knowledge is superior to mathematical knowledge.[4]

A DILEMMA CONCERNING THE STATUS OF MOTION	
Is Motion Real?	**Problem**
Yes	Contradicts the mathematical fact that there are an infinite number of points between any two places.
No	Contradicts our common sense belief that motion is real.

Exercise
2. Come up with a reason why it might be problematic to claim that perceptual knowledge is superior to mathematical knowledge. Similarly explain why it might be problematic to claim that mathematical knowledge is superior to perceptual knowledge.

Zeno's Paradox and Rational Criticism

Zeno's paradox reveals that our view of the world is deeply problematic. In light of this problem, Zeno argued that the theory of the dynamicists, which asserted the possibility of motion across distances, was mistaken since it contradicted our mathematical understanding of distances. If *we* are going to respond to Zeno's problem in a philosophical way, in a way that constitutes rational criticism, then we need to construct a theory that remedies the problem. You are now aware of at least two such remedies: Zeno's theory that *motion is an illusion*, and the dynamicists theory that *the mathematical representation of distance is mistaken*. Which response do you sympathize with? Do you believe, as Pythagoras and Zeno did, that Reality conforms to the results of mathematics *even when these results fly in the face of ordinary experience*? Or do you believe, as the dynamicists did, that Reality conforms to some of our everyday perceptions, *even when these perceptions fly in the face of basic mathematical concepts*?

Democritus, a dynamicist who was aware of Zeno's paradox, responded to this problem by turning away from mathematical results, and by arguing that Reality consisted of

---

[4]For further discussion of logical strategy in the face of paradox or contradiction, see "Logic and Personal Identity" in Chapter 15 below.

merely atoms and empty space. By claiming that atoms were in motion *by nature*, Democritus formulated a theory that flew in the face of basic mathematical concepts. Zeno, to be sure, would not have sympathized with Democritus' response. Here is an imaginary conversation between the two men:

> DEMOCRITUS: Motion is real.
>
> ZENO: No. Your theory is wrong. We do perceive things in motion, but motion is an illusion. For, motion always occurs between two points. But between any two points there are an infinite number points, and nothing can traverse an infinite number points in a finite amount of time. Motion, therefore, is an illusion.
>
> DEMOCRITUS: You are wrong, Zeno! Everything is made of atoms. Atoms are in motion. Motion, therefore, must be real.
>
> ZENO: You obviously did not pay attention to my argument. Even worse, your response assumes what I have proved cannot be true with my paradox. My view is to be favored over yours, for yours is at odds with mathematics, our most exact science! You have failed to convince me that I am mistaken in my proof that motion is an illusion.

Exercise
3.   Is Democritus reacting in a way that constitutes rational criticism? Explain why you think Democritus is responding in the "mystical," "rational," "philosophical" or some other way.

Protagoras and the Sophists: The Way of Relativism

Can We Know the Nature of Reality?
So far you have seen that although philosophers generally agree that appearances are not reality, there is disagreement concerning the nature of Reality. Let us review the theories of Reality that have been thus far discussed:

> Thales: Everything is Water
> Anaximander: Everything is Infinite Boundless
> Anaximenes: Everything is Air
> Rational Pythagoreans: Everything is made of Rational Numbers
> Philosophical Pythagoreans: Everything is made of Rational and
> Irrational Numbers
> Parmenides and Zeno: Everything is One; motion is illusory
> Heraclitus: Everything is logos and change
> Democritus: Everything is atoms and empty space
> *Your view* : _____

The fact that there is so much disagreement about the subject could very well lead one to conclude that we really can't know anything about the nature of Reality. This is roughly what the Sophist Gorgias believed. Recall his argument:
(i) If anything is, it is incomprehensible and unknowable.

(ii) Even if something was comprehensible and knowable, it would be incommunicable.

Therefore,

(iii) nothing is.

According to Gorgias, nothing is -- not even truth! And even if there were truth, we neither could know it, nor communicate it. What is the true theory of Reality? Even if it is one of the theories listed above, or even if it is Gorgias', at best it could not be communicated. But then we would be wasting out time to talk about it. End of discussion.

Protagoras' Bucket Experiment

Protagoras' argument is certainly a more active criticism of those who claim that we can know the absolute truth about Reality. In performing his bucket experiment, Protagoras took the first step in rationally criticizing the views of the Milesians, the Pythagoreans, the dynamicists, the staticists, and any other philosopher who believes in an absolute, objective truth. In taking a somewhat "mystical" second step, Protagoras concluded from his experiment that there is no truth apart from human experience. Thus, if you feel that the water is cold, then, relative to you, it is true that the water is cold, and if someone else feels that the water is hot, then, relative to that person, it is true that the water is hot. Who is *really* right? According to Protagoras this is a nonsensical question, for it assumes that truth transcends human experience. Protagoras thinks that this is the wrong way to understand truth.

But does Protagoras propose an alternative theory? Maybe. You decide. Recall the following passage:

> ...These appearances some [people], through inexperience, call "true"; but I say that some [appearances] are "better" than others, not "truer." And the wise, friend Socrates, I am far from calling frogs, but when they have to do with the body I call them physicians, and when they have to do with plants, farmers. For I maintain that the latter induce in sickly plants good and healthy and true[5] sensations instead of bad...

In claiming that experts can bring about desirable states in their relevant objects of expertise, Protagoras *shifts the discussion* of a Reality that transcends human appearances, to a discussion about how to make the appearances *healthy*.

In order to see how Protagoras moves in a direction markedly different from the philosophers discussed thus far, note the difference between knowing *that* something is so-and-so, on the one hand, and knowing *how* to use that knowledge, on the other. The Milesians, the Pythagoreans, the staticists and the dynamicists, all place emphasis on the mode of "knowing that," while they de-emphasize the mode of "knowing how." These philosophers were primarily concerned with formulating the correct theory of Reality, rather than knowing how to *use* such a theory. Protagoras, however, places primary importance on the mode of "knowing how," while he de-emphasizes the mode of "knowing that." Indeed, by arguing that truth is *relative* to the individual (via the bucket experiment), Protagoras de-emphasizes the mode of "knowing that." According to Protagoras, knowing that such-and-such is the case, is not as important as knowing how to improve things. Or maybe he thinks that knowing that such-and-such, in some sense, *amounts to* knowing how to improve things.

---

[5] Why do you think Protagoras chooses to use the word "true" (Greek: "aleitheia") here? Note that he uses it to describe the sensations of plants. This is clearly not how the term is normally used.

Exercises

1.   In proposing that the mode of "knowing how" is more important than the mode of "knowing that," do you think that Protagoras engages in the second step of rational criticism? In other words, do you think that Protagoras proposes a positive theory that is immune to the criticisms that he raises against philosophers like Zeno, Pythagoras, and Democritus? (By "positive theory," we mean a theory that affirms something versus simply denying some other theory.) Explain your answer.

2.   In your own words, briefly summarize the -ism (discussed in §1.8 of *Lovers of Wisdom*), and name the philosopher(s) that advocated it:
(i) Epistemological relativism
(ii) Epistemological objectivism
(iii) Conventionalism
(iv) Moral relativism
(v) Epistemological nihilism
(vi) Epistemological skepticism
(vii) Epistemological authoritarianism

Chapter 2

Plato

Plato's *Euthyphro*

You saw that Euthyphro took himself to be an expert on "piety," but could not provide an unproblematic definition of the term. These were his attempts at defining "piety."

Attempt 1: Piety is doing what I am doing, prosecuting my father.
Attempt 2: Piety is what is dear to the gods.
Attempt 3: Piety is what is loved by all the gods.
Attempt 4: Piety is the part of justice that is a sort of ministration to the gods.
Attempt 5: Piety is what is pleasing to the gods in word and deed.

Exercise

1. Socrates pointed out the problems with each of these definitions. To make sure you understand why Socrates criticized each of these answers, write down *in your own words* what you take to be Socrates' criticisms of each of Euthyphro's attempts:

2. Why would Socrates be so confrontational as to refute each of Euthyphro's answers. After reading the *Apology*, perhaps you think that Socrates refutes Euthyphro in order to show that Euthyphro is really *un*wise. For it was Socrates' god-given mission to expose the ignorance of people who wrongly claimed to be wise. But this just pushes the question back. Why would the god assign such a mission? What is the value in showing someone who believes that they are wise, that they really are *un*wise?

Rationally Criticizing Euthyphro's Definition of "Piety"

Rational criticism, as you have learned, involves two steps: first, the limitations of a theory are made explicit, and then a new theory is proposed that seems to be free from these limitations. Thinking of each of Euthyphro's definition-attempts as a *theory* about the nature of "piety," Socrates' criticisms can be seen as satisfying the first step of rational criticism. For Socrates indeed makes explicit the limitations inherent in each of Euthyphro's "theories." Importantly, however, Socrates often shows that Euthyphro's theory is problematic *because his theory is not consonant with Euthyphro's other beliefs.* For instance, Socrates shows that Euthyphro's definition of "piety" as "what is dear to the gods" is mistaken due to Euthyphro's belief that the gods disagree on what things are "dear." For Euthyphro's definition, in conjunction with his belief that the gods *have* this disagreement, entails that some things are both pious and impious.

Clearly, this is not an adequate answer to Socrates' question. Socrates, if you remember, wanted Euthyphro to say what is the one thing common to *all and only* pious (or holy) things. Euthyphro's definition, in conjunction with some of his other beliefs, unfortunately, encompasses both "holy" *and* "unholy" things. So, Socrates engaged Euthyphro in the first step of rational criticism in a particular way that made use of Euthyphro's other beliefs. But, did Socrates engage Euthyphro in the second step of rational criticism? Did Socrates get Euthyphro to offer a positive new theory? It is true that even after several attempts, Euthyphro failed to articulate an unproblematic definition of "piety." But does this fact entail that Euthyphro failed to advance his understanding of "piety?" In order to see why the answer to this question is "no," let us recreate the process in which Euthyphro was engaged.

Exercise
3.   What is the one thing common to all and only tables? Think about this for a few minutes, then write down your answer.

Perhaps you wrote down something like "What is common to all and only tables is having four legs and a flat surface." If you did, your answer is problematic. For, on the one hand, defining "tablehood" as "having four legs and a flat surface" implies that *all* tables have these characteristics. So, according to this definition there are no one-legged tables, and this, of course, is false (there are some tables that are supported by a single stand). On the other hand, defining "tablehood" as "having four legs and a flat surface" implies that *only* tables have four legs and a flat surface. But this too is false. For instance, the desks typically found in classrooms have four legs and a flat surface but are not tables.

How Definitions can be Faulty
We have illustrated two ways that an attempted definition of a term can fail to "pick out" or describe all and only things to which that term applies: (i) the definition can fail to apply to *all* of the relevant things (e.g. our definition of "tablehood" does not apply to all things which are tables since it does not apply to one-legged tables), and (ii) the definition can fail to apply to *only* the relevant things (e.g. our definition of "tablehood" applies to classroom desks, which are not tables). In the one case, therefore, our definition of "tablehood" falls short of the mark by leaving out some tables, and in the other case the definition overshoots the mark by including some things which are not tables. In the former case we say that the definition is *too narrow*, and in the latter case we say that the definition is *too broad*.

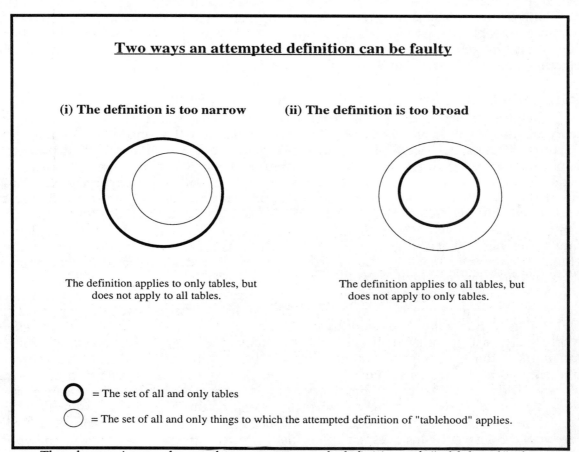

Two ways an attempted definition can be faulty

(i) The definition is too narrow

(ii) The definition is too broad

The definition applies to only tables, but does not apply to all tables.

The definition applies to all tables, but does not apply to only tables.

= The set of all and only tables

= The set of all and only things to which the attempted definition of "tablehood" applies.

The above picture shows that an attempted definition of "tablehood" that is too narrow, applies to only tables, but does not apply to all tables. An attempted definition of "tablehood" that is too broad, on the other hand, applies to all tables, but does not apply to only tables. In both cases the attempted definition is *partly* right. Many tables do have four legs and a flat surface, so we want our definition of "tablehood" to include *some* things which fit this description, but not all and only those things. To this extent, the attempt is not just an error, but a "first approximation" which can be developed into a definition which hits the mark.

Exercises:

4.   Above we discussed how a faulty definition can be either too broad or too narrow. But, a definition can also be faulty because it is too broad *and* too narrow. Recall our definition of "tablehood" as "having four legs and a flat surface." This definition is too narrow since it does not encompass tables that have a single support. Moreover, this definition is too broad since implies that non-tables (e.g., desks) are, in fact, tables. Below, draw your own diagram illustrating what it would be for a definition to be both too broad *and* too narrow.

How a definition can be both too broad and too narrow

(iii) Too broad and too narrow

○ = The set of all and only tables

○ = The set of all and only things to which the attempted definition of "tablehood" applies

Rationally Criticizing Your Definition of "tablehood"

5.   Now, write down a counterexample to your definition of "tablehood" (given in 3 above) that shows that it is either too broad, too narrow, or both.

6.   In completing exercises 3 and 5, you have performed the first step of rational criticism: you have found a limitation in your "theory" of tablehood. Now that you are aware that your definition is problematic, take the next step in the process of rational criticism: formulate another definition that is immune to the counterexample which you have discovered.

In exercise 3 you gave an attempted definition of tablehood, in exercise 5 you performed the first step of rational criticism by finding a counterexample to this definition, and in exercise 6 you performed the second step of rational criticism by proposing a better theory. To be sure, "tablehood" is an uninteresting notion to define. But it is the process upon which you should be focused. The *process* of attempt/counterexample/re-attempt is perhaps our most powerful instrument for learning about ourselves and the world.

The Value of Rational Criticism

Remember that we recreated the process in which Euthyphro was engaged in order to illustrate that, despite the fact that Euthyphro was unable to formulate an adequate definition of "piety," he nonetheless deepened his understanding of the term. But how can engaging in rational criticism be valuable even if it does not lead to a completely unproblematic theory? Before you engaged in this activity, you had a relatively vague notion of "tablehood." In repeatedly attempting to define the term, however, your concept became more precise. It got closer to hitting the mark. Not only were you forced to think about what "tablehood" consists in, but you also became more aware of which characteristics are and which are not necessarily involved in the notion of "tablehood." By subjecting your definitions of "tablehood" to rational criticism, your conception of "tablehood" became sharper, clearer, better. You have a better understanding of the concept. Furthermore, in subjecting your concepts to rational criticism, you become aware of what you do not know. You don't yet know the essence of a table. And being aware of what you do not know is a necessary condition of human wisdom.

Now, when important notions like piety, personhood, existence, virtue, space, time, God, etc. are subjected to rational criticism, we deepen our understanding of ourselves and the world. We also come to realize our own limitations, what we do and do not know. Importantly, however, this deepened understanding brings with it, a *change in our behavior*. Indeed, Diogenes Laertius (one of our ancient sources) tells us that after conversing with Socrates, Euthyphro decided *not* to prosecute his father. Because he had deepened his understanding of "piety," and because he became aware of what he did not know, Euthyphro reasoned that prosecuting his father might very well be *impious*. Euthyphro's actions were indeed affected by his deepened understanding of "piety." Socrates, wanting to engage others in rational criticism, sought to deepen his interlocutor's understanding of moral terms, and hence to help them engage in more moral behavior.

Plato's *Parmenides*

The Relationship Between Forms and Predicates

Plato articulates his theory of ideal forms in the *Parmenides*. This dialog especially illustrates Plato's love for rational criticism. Plato has the character of Parmenides criticize the theory of forms. One can begin to understand the nature of Plato's forms by showing how they correspond to *language*.

Plato's forms - or ideas -- are conceptually related to linguistic units which are called *predicates*. What is a predicate? Predicates are "general" terms which pick out *many* individuals, in contradistinction to *singular terms* which pick out a *single* individual. For instance, look at the following simple sentence:

Michael Jordan is a man.

"Michael Jordan" which is the subject of the sentence, of course refers to a single, unique individual, and therefore is a singular term.[6] "is a man," however, which is the predicate of the above sentence, picks out *many* individuals. In order to see this, note that "_____ is man" could be filled in with many *different* things that would cause the sentence to be true. So, we say that whereas singular terms are *singularly instantiated* (since they refer to one individual), predicates are *multiply instantiated* (since they refer to many).

You are already familiar with one of the questions prompted by the existence of multiply instantiated terms. A collection of *different* things, of different beautiful things for instance, prompts the question "what is common to all and only beautiful things?" Similarly, a collection of different books, prompts the question, "what is common to all and only books?" It indeed seems that in order to answer such a question, we must abstract from all of the *differences* among beautiful things, among books, in order to get to the *common characteristic*

---

[6] In addition to proper names, *definite descriptions* are also kinds of singular terms. Definite descriptions usually involve the definite article "the" -- e.g., "the author of *Lovers of Wisdom*."

which they all share. When dealing with predicates like "is beautiful" and "is pious," it becomes quite difficult to do this. In some cases, for instance, it is the very thing that makes something *different* from the others of its kind that makes it either beautiful or pious.

Plato's theory of ideal forms provides an answer to Socrates' difficult question "What is F-ness?" It provides an answer to questions like "what is common to all beautiful things?" and "what is common to all pious things?" According to Plato, all beautiful things partake in the *form (or idea) of beauty*, just as all pious things partake in the *form (or idea) of piety*. Moreover, Plato claims that the ideal forms of beauty and piety, are respectively beautiful and pious. Indeed, if neither the form of beauty was beautiful, nor the form of piety was pious, from where would beautiful things receive their beauty, from where would pious things receive their piety?

Rationally Criticizing Plato's Theory of Forms

In the *Parmenides*, Plato depicts Parmenides discovering a flaw in the theory of ideal forms. Recall Parmenides' observation that this theory entails the undesirable consequence that there are an *infinite number* of forms corresponding to a common characteristic:

> PARMENIDES: I imagine that your reason for assuming one idea for each kind is as follows: whenever a number of objects appear to you to be great, there doubtless seems to you to be one and the same idea visible in them all, hence, you conceive greatness as one.

> SOCRATES: Very true.

> PARMENIDES: But now, if you allow your mind in like manner to embrace in one view this *real greatness* and these other great things, will not one more greatness arise, being required for the semblance of all of these?

> SOCRATES: It would seem so.

> PARMENIDES: Then another idea of greatness comes into view and above absolute greatness and the individuals which partake of it, and then another over and above these, by virtue of which they will all be great, and so you will be left not with a single idea in every case, but an infinite number.

What is the criticism of Plato's theory of ideal forms? We can see that it turns on the assumption that corresponding to each multiply instantiated term like "great," is a unique idea. Given the collection of all great things, for instance, Plato assumes that there must be a single idea of greatness in which each member of that collection partakes. The crunch comes when we consider Plato's claim that the idea of greatness is *also* a great thing. For this assumption entails that the idea of greatness, since it is a great thing, is a member of the collection of all great things.

To make Parmenides' argument more perspicuous, imagine that there are only seven great things in the entire world: the seven ancient wonders of the world. Plato believes that since "greatness" is multiply instantiated (in our example it is instantiated seven times), there must be an idea of greatness in which all of these instances "partake:"

1. The Pyramids of Giza
2. The Hanging Gardens of Babylon
3. The Shrine of Zeus at Olympia
4. The Mausoleum of Mycerinus
5. The Temple of Artemis at Ephesus
6. The Colossus of Rhodes
7. The Lighthouse at Faros

THE IDEA OF
GREATNESS

But the idea of greatness, claims Plato, is itself a "great thing," and this implies that there are not seven great things, but *eight*. Yet, if there are eight great things, then greatness is multiply instantiated, and we need another idea of greatness, "greatness^2," that subsumes the eight great things: the idea of greatness, and the seven wonders of the world.

1. The Pyramids of Giza
2. The Hanging Gardens of Babylon
3. The Shrine of Zeus at Olympia
4. The Mausoleum of Mycerinus
5. The Temple of Artemis at Ephesus
6. The Colossus of Rhodes
7. The Lighthouse at Faros
8. The form of greatness

GREATNESS^2

But of course, now there are not eight great things but *nine* (since greatness^2 is also great), and so on *ad infinitum*.

Plato's answer to the question "what is the one thing common to all and only great things," like each of Euthyphro's answers, is clearly problematic. Now, however, you know why Plato subjected his views to criticism. Concerned with an interesting philosophical question, Plato, by engaging in rational criticism, advanced his understanding of the matter. And by writing a dialogue in which his own views are criticized, Plato gives us another way of expressing his love for rational criticism.

Exercise
7. As a final exercise, think about the natures of things. In other words, what makes a thing "beautiful," "courageous," "valuable," or "great," if Plato's answer is wrong? If it is not because they partake in an idea of some sort, then what is it? What is the essence of a beautiful thing, the common characteristic to all and only beautiful items? Courageous things? Valuable things? What is the one thing that makes us put them in the category that we put them in? Plato admits to us that his theory of forms is not without difficulties, so what are the answers to these questions? If you *really* want to know, you now know what to do.

Chapter 3

Aristotle

Aristotle's concept of substance has influenced the whole of western philosophy. It was developed in opposition to Plato's theory of ideas. In this chapter, we will review Aristotle's rational criticism of Plato's theory and examine the alternative that he proposes, the theory of "substance." We will then be in a much better position to understand much of the western philosophy that followed him.

Although Aristotle had several criticisms of Plato's theory of ideas, perhaps his most devastating and well known is the *third man argument*. This argument is a version of the one raised by Parmenides. If there are many men, then, according to Plato's theory of ideas, there must be the idea of manhood that is common to them all. But, this idea must itself exhibit the property of manhood. In other words, on Plato's view, the idea of manhood is manly. Since there is now a larger set of things which exhibit the property manhood (the set of all men plus the idea of manhood itself), it follows that there must be a new form which subsumes this larger set. This process can be carried out *ad infinitum*. So, if we posit an idea corresponding to each predicate, then one is forced to posit an infinity of ideas corresponding to each predicate. Aristotle takes this to be a sufficient reason for rejecting Plato's theory of ideas altogether, and offers his theory of substance in its place.

Substance: Aristotle's Alternative to Plato's Forms

In the second step of rational criticism, recall, one proposes a theory that seems to be less problematic than the one originally proposed. Parmenides satisfied the second step of rational criticism by denying that "the many" existed, and by arguing instead that reality is One. Aristotle, on the other hand, does not satisfy the second step of rational criticism in this way. Instead of modifying Plato's theory in some minor way to avoid the third man criticism, he provides a radically different alternative. Aristotle not only provides an alternative theory that is free from the third man criticism, he addresses the *initial* problem which Plato's theory attempted to solve (the relation between the universal and the particular). His solution involves one of the most important metaphysical concepts in the history of western philosophy, the concept of *substance*.

Recall the distinction between predicates and singular terms discussed in Chapter 2. Predicates are "general" terms that pick out *many* individuals, in contradistinction to *singular terms* each of which pick out a *single* individual. The predicate "is a man," for example, picks out many individuals (Michael Jordan, Bill Clinton, Martin Luther King Jr., etc.). On the other hand, the singular terms "Michael Jordan," "Bill Clinton," and "Martin Luther King Jr.," each refer to a unique individual.

We saw that Platonic forms (say, of "greatness") correspond to a predicates since many things (such as the seven ancient wonders of the world) partake in them. Plato, moreover, believed that forms were the ultimate constituents of reality. Thus, for Plato, the Real is composed of abstract entities -- the form of greatness (which itself exhibits greatness), and of manhood (which is itself "manly"), and so on for the rest of the ideas.

On Aristotle's view, however, such a scenario is impossible. According to Aristotle, although abstract entities like "greatness," and "manhood" are real, their existence is nevertheless *abstracted from* particular great things and particular men.[7] According to Aristotle, the ultimate constituents of reality are not abstract entities, but are particular,

---

[7]We will examine Aristotle's notion of abstraction in more detail in Chapter 6.

concrete entities -- things that are denoted by *singular terms*. Recall Aristotle's remark from the *Categories*:

> Substance, in the truest and **primary**...sense of the word...is that which is [not] predicable of a subject; for instance, the individual man or horse. But in a **secondary** sense those things are called substances within which, as species, the primary substances are included; also those which, as genera, include the species. For instance, the individual man is included in the species "man," and the genus to which the species belongs is "animal"; ...the species "man" and the genus "animal" are termed secondary substances.

Primary versus Secondary Substances

The distinction between primary and secondary substances marks a crucial difference between Aristotle's view of Reality and Plato's. Primary substances do not correspond to abstract things like "greatness" and "beauty," but to particular great or beautiful things. This is what Aristotle means when he says that primary substance is not "predicable of a subject." Primary substances, in other words, do not correspond to predicates, but to singular terms. In contrast, secondary substances such as "man" and "animal," *can* function as predicates. This is what Aristotle means when he says that, "both the name and the definition of the species are predicable of the individual." However, secondary substances can only function as predicates in a qualified way. A substance can only function as a predicate if that substance is "more general" than that of which it is predicated.

	GENUS [e.g., Animal]
SECONDARY SUBSTANCES	
	SPECIES [e.g., Man]
PRIMARY SUBSTANCE	**INDIVIDUAL** [e.g., Bill Clinton]

We can say things like "man is an animal," and hence predicate "animalhood" of "man." For "animalhood" is more general than "manhood." Similarly, we can say "Bill Clinton is a man," and hence predicate "manhood" of Bill Clinton. Accordingly, "manhood" is more general than "Bill Clinton." However, and this is the important part, we cannot say things like "Man is a Bill Clinton." For "Bill Clinton" is not more general than "manhood." This is what Aristotle has in mind when he claims that *primary substance is not predicable of a subject*. A primary substance is the ultimate particular, and hence is never general. So a primary substance can never function as a predicate. Only *secondary* substances can.

Why Aristotle's Theory of Substance is Immune to the Third Man Argument

Why is Aristotle's theory of substance immune to the third man argument? In the argument, there are two propositions that entail the undesirable consequence that "an infinite number of ideas corresponds to a single predicate." If we use "F" as a variable ranging over properties, then we can represent these two propositions as:

(i) there must be an idea of F which makes all F things F's, and

(ii) the idea of F itself exhibits F-ness.

It is the second assumption in virtue of which sentences like "manhood is manly" are meaningful, and it is the second assumption that Aristotle denies. Since a substance can function as a predicate only if that substance is more general than that which it is predicating, sentences like "manhood is manly" are meaningless. Such sentences violate Aristotle's strictures on predication: "man" -- a species -- can only be predicated of a substance *less general* than "man." In the sentence "manhood is manly," however, the predicate "manly" is *not* more general than "manhood." Both "manhood" and "manly," are equally general.

If you are having trouble understanding why Aristotle's doctrine of substance is immune to the third man argument, try to generate the third man argument without the assumption that, for example, manhood is manly. As you should see, without this assumption, the argument cannot be formulated. Aristotle's theory of substance is immune to the third man argument because it involves a theory of predication in which sentences like "manhood is manly" are ungrammatical, and hence meaningless.

The Components of Substance: Form and Matter

Aristotle's notion of substance is important not only because it is immune to the third man argument, but also because it enables Aristotle to account for both the *essences* that primary substances seem to exhibit, and the *change* to which such substances are subject. Let us see how the notion of "substance" can account for both essence and change. Recall the following passage from *On the Soul* (see *Lovers of Wisdom* Chapter 3.3):

> Now there is one class of existent things which we call substance, including under the term, firstly, matter, which in itself is not this or that; secondly, ...form, in virtue of which the terms "this" or "that" are applied.; thirdly, the whole made up of matter and form.

Substances, as we mentioned above, can either be particular entities -- such as Bill Clinton and Michael Jordan, or, the species and genera of a particular entity such as "animal" and "man." In the above passage, however, Aristotle also tells us that there are three *kinds* of substance: (i) matter, (ii) form and (iii) the combination of matter and form. All primary substances, according to Aristotle, are instances of the third type of substance. And hence all concrete entities are composed of matter and form. Since "form" and "matter" are not concrete entities, they are both instances of secondary substances.

SUBSTANCE	
<u>Primary</u>	<u>Secondary</u>
form+matter	form, matter

It is by understanding primary substances as having both formal and material aspects, which enables Aristotle to account for both the essences of primary substances, and the change to which they are subject.

Let's say a bit about the formal and material aspects of a primary substance. Aristotle notices that all primary substances -- whether they are animate like plants and animals, or inanimate like axes and chairs, have both *essential* and *accidental* characteristics. For instance, being a person is part of your essence, but reading this book is not; it just so happens that you are reading this book, and eventually you will be doing something else. Importantly, Aristotle ties the essential characteristics of a primary substance to its *formal* aspect. The formal aspect of a living thing is its *soul,* and the formal aspect of an inanimate substance is its *function*.[8]   On the other hand, Aristotle ties the accidental characteristics of a primary substance to its *material* aspect.   A particular man may be 5'9, speak Greek, and so on, but these characteristics are not essential to the soul of man. Similarly, a particular ax may have a wooden handle, 12 inch blade, and so on, but these features are not essential to the *function* of the ax.   Characteristics that are accidental to both animate and inanimate substances, are features of the material component of these substances.

Substance and Change

Aristotle uses the fact that primary substances have both formal and material components, to account for the *change* to which such substances are subject.   Unlike Plato, who thought the world of change and becoming was illusory, Aristotle believed that change was very real.   According to Aristotle, there are at least two kinds of change: (i) a type of change peculiar to living things and (ii) a type of change that both living and non-living things undergo. The first type is the change that is characteristic of development and growth (think of an acorn changing into an oak tree, a baby changing into an adult, etc.).   On the other hand, things can change without growing -- you change the color of your car, your hair, etc.   This is the second type of change.   Thus Aristotle thinks that there is both *developmental* and *incidental* change.   Aristotle uses his form/matter dichotomy in order to explain both kinds of change.

According to Aristotle, the form of an organism governs its development.   Think of the form of an organism as containing information, information which animates and controls the organism   -- information that takes some time to be communicated to the matter. Developmental change is simply the change that the matter undergoes upon "receiving the information" from the form.   In other words, while the form -- which does not change -- communicates to the matter, the matter responds by changing.   In developmental change, therefore, form dictates the change, and matter submits.   Think of a sculptor working on marble.   Like the form, the sculptor dictates the change to the matter, and the matter yields, complies, obeys.   This is how Aristotle uses the form/matter dichotomy to account for developmental change.

How does Aristotle's form/matter dichotomy describe incidental change?   Think of a wooden chair that is painted from white to black.   Since the chair is a particular thing, and hence an individual substance, it has both form and matter, and hence both essential and accidental characteristics.   Essential to the chair is its function, and it is the form of "chair" that dictates this function.[9] On the other hand, the wood out of which the chair is made, the matter, is only accidentally white; it could be some other color and still be *wood*.   And the accidental characteristics of this substance may be replaced with others without disrupting its organization.   Just as it does in developmental change, matter submits to the same form (function, in the case of the chair) while accepting a diversity of accidental characteristics (such as color).   This is how Aristotle uses the form/matter dichotomy to account for incidental change.

Concluding

As a theory which blocks the third man argument, Aristotle's notion of substance, including the form/matter dichotomy, has the additional virtue of accounting for the apparent essences of things, and, moreover, of solving the problem of change. Because of the elegance of this theory, it remained virtually unscathed until the eighteenth century, when it was attacked first by Berkeley, and then by Hume.   Engaging in rational criticism, Berkeley and Hume replaced theories containing Aristotelian assumptions with theories that they believed were less problematic.   Look for Aristotle's notion of substance (in some cases altered) when you read the Medieval philosophers, Descartes, Locke, Berkeley, Hume and Leibniz.   In the meantime, a question to ask yourself is "what aspect of substance is more real, substance *as form* , substance *as matter*, or the combination of the two?"   Aristotle wrestled with this

---

[8]The notion of the form of inanimate things will be extended to more than function in Chapter 6.
[9]Remember that this is not the Platonic form "chairhood."

question and never adequately answered it. He seems to suggest at times that the *form* of substance has ontological primacy. This, indeed, is reminiscent of Plato's philosophy, but there are nonetheless important differences between these two men. We leave it to you to make explicit to yourself these differences, and to ask yourself whether you take Aristotle's or Plato's theory to be more persuasive.

Chapter 4

The Epicureans and Stoics

What Causes Your Pain?

Sigmund Freud, the founder of modern psychology, has been said to have introduced himself to strangers with the question, "who are you and why do you lie?" In like manner, we begin this chapter with the question, "who are you and why are you *disturbed*?" Think of some disturbing and painful experience you have had (the very most disturbing and painful experience you've ever had, if you can bear it), and complete the exercise below.

Exercise

1.   Try to identify *why* you experienced the disturbance and pain. In other words, write down the cause(s) of this pain. Make sure that you record your answer below, as you will be referring to it later.

You probably answered the above by explaining that certain *events* were the cause of your pain. Many events, however, are things that happen to us, things of which we are not in control. A loved one dies in a tragic accident, you are hurt, but the event was not in your control. You learn about some of the horrors that once befell mankind -- the Holocaust and Hiroshima, for example -- you are hurt, but these events were not in your control. If you believe that pain is primarily caused by events of which you are not in control, then it is virtually impossible for you to be guarded from pain. How then, in the face of unrelenting pain, are you supposed to live a peaceful and happy life? It seems hopeless.

The philosophers about whom you read in Chapter 4 of *Lovers of Wisdom*, the Epicureans, Skeptics, and Stoics, all deny that uncontrollable events are the primary causes of pain. Instead, they say that certain cognitive states -- states that we can control -- are the main causes of pain. The Epicureans, Skeptics and Stoics, moreover, also provide theories that explain how to *engineer* these states so that they cease to be causes of pain. And so, the possibility of happy life seems to emerge. Let us review.

Epicurus

In order to appreciate the philosophy of Epicurus, one must be mindful of the views that were commonplace during the time in which he was writing. The majority of men and women who lived during this time, save a handful of philosophers, believed that gods and goddesses, Zeus, Athena, and Apollo, for example, were jealous of one another, were deceitful, and were responsible for events that transpired on earth. Homer's *Iliad*, although written several hundred years before the time of Epicurus, is studded with instances of the gods intervening, albeit discommodiously, in human affairs. In the following passage, Homer describes how Zeus intervenes in the war between the Greeks and the Trojans. Because he so loves the Trojans, Zeus causes trouble for Ajax, one of the Greeks' most powerful warriors:

> Hektor [a Trojan] stood up close to Ajax and hacked at the ash spear with his great sword, striking behind the socket of the spearhead, and slashed it clean away, so that Ajax shook there in his hand with a lopped spear...and Ajax knew in his blameless heart, and shivered for knowing it, how this was gods' work, how

> Zeus cut across the intention in all his battle, how he planned that
> the Trojans should conquer.[10]

Because the ancient Greeks believed that gods and goddesses intervened in the lives of men and women in disadvantageous ways, the ancient gods and goddesses were commonly feared.

Although our conception of God differs markedly from that of the ancients', the Greeks were nevertheless familiar with the concept of an afterlife. And, as were the gods and goddesses, the afterlife was feared by many. Cephalus' remark from Plato's *Republic* illustrates:

> ...when a man begins to realize that he is going to die, he is filled
> with apprehensions.... The tales that are told of the world below
> and how the men who have done wrong must pay the penalty
> there...begin to torture his soul.[11]

Observing that many people were disturbed by thinking about both the gods and death, Epicurus reasoned that *beliefs*, rather than events, were the main sources of pain (of all kinds). In particular, Epicurus thought that beliefs about gods, about death, and beliefs that were not the products of reason, were the main causes of pain. Recall the passage from Epicurus' *Letter to Herodotus* in *Lovers of Wisdom*:

> the principal disturbance in the minds of men arises because they
> think that these celestial bodies are blessed and immortal, and yet
> have wills ...inconsistent with these attributes; and because they
> are always expecting or imagining some everlasting misery ... or
> even fear...death... and...because they are brought to this...not by
> reasoned opinion, but rather by some [arrational] presentiment...

Exercise
2.   In light of Epicurus' view that certain kinds of beliefs are the main sources of pain, let's return to your answer to exercise 1. Try to modify your description of what caused your pain by *redescribing* the cause in terms of beliefs. For example, if you originally answered that "unrequited love" was the cause of a disturbing experience, you could redescribe this discomfort as being caused by a belief that "if my love is unrequited, then I am undesirable."

You should now be aware of certain of your beliefs that you suspect are pain-causing. Let us then see what Epicurus recommends for such beliefs.

Philosophy!? The Cure for Pain?
If beliefs about either the gods or death cause you pain, Epicurus recommends *philosophy*. Why? Philosophy can purge us of superstitions and change those beliefs which cause pain. In particular, it is the philosophy of the atomists (e.g., Democritus), by which we can realize that there is no reason to fear either the gods or death. Once we understand atomistic philosophy, claims Epicurus, we will realize that the gods are not responsible for events on earth, and so, we will no longer fear them. Events in the world, then, are not caused by the wills of transcendent beings, but are rather caused *mechanically*, and consist in a sequence of cause/effect relationships involving only things -- conglomerations of atoms -- on earth. Ajax, for example, did not die in battle because he was being avenged by Zeus, but rather because his physiological constitution could not withstand the injuries that he suffered. Nor did Ajax need to fear death upon the battlefield. For atomism teaches us that the soul is nothing but a conglomeration of atoms. Upon death the soul-atoms disperse, and there is thus no subject present to feel death. Death is a nothingness, and therefore there is no *something* to

---

[10]From book 16 (115). The translation is from Richard Lattimore's *The Iliad of Homer* (1951 Chicago.)
[11] Book I (330a-331a) in Plato's *Republic*. The translation is Paul Shorey's.

fear and no *something* to do the fearing. Once we understand that we do not, indeed cannot, experience death, beliefs concerning death become disarmed.

Thus, if you are disturbed by beliefs about either the gods or death, Epicurus recommends atomistic philosophy as a remedy. However, even if Epicurus is right to say that certain beliefs are the main causes of pain, and even if he is right to recommend atomistic philosophy as a therapy for beliefs about the gods and about death, it is unlikely that *you* are pained by these sorts of beliefs. Thus, it is unlikely that your pain will be remedied by pursuing atomistic philosophy. Nonetheless, perhaps your pain-causing beliefs are "arrational,"[12] insofar as they are not products of reason, of rational reflection. If so, Epicurus has some advice.

Philosophy and rational activity, according to Epicurus, can transform arrational beliefs into rational beliefs that are innocent of causing pain. In other words, if arrational beliefs are the main causes of pain, then pursuing philosophy and rational activity is a way of *treating* our beliefs, of engineering them, so that they cease to be sources of anything but minor discomforts. In his *Letter to Herodotus*, Epicurus writes:

> because [the many] are brought to [pain] not by reasoned opinion, but...by some [arrational] presentiment...they do not know the limits of pain... [and] suffer a disturbance equally great or even more extensive than if they had reached this belief by [reasoned] opinion...Wherefore we must pay attention to internal feelings and to external sensations...and to every immediate intuition in accordance with each of the standards of judgment.

If arrational beliefs are causing you pain, philosophy is the cure. Why? Through philosophy, claims Epicurus, we can view the experience of pain *objectively*, rather than *subjectively*. By pursuing philosophy we can come to know the principles by which all phenomena are to be judged, and when we understand pain in light of these principles, we can see pain for what it is, master it, and not be controlled by it. By changing our beliefs through philosophical reflection we can change the *mode of presentation* of the events we experience, the *way* the events we experience present themselves to us, e.g. as painful, or pleasurable, or neither, etc. As Socrates' interrogation of Euthyphro's view of "piety" modified Euthyphro's understanding of pious things (recall Chapter 2), subjecting views about "pain" to philosophical scrutiny, can modify our understanding of pain.

According to Epicurus then, if you are disturbed by arrational beliefs, such as beliefs about the gods or beliefs about death, then philosophy should be pursued. But what if the beliefs by which you are disturbed are not arrational? What if Epicurus fails to describe a therapy for the kind of beliefs by which *you* are troubled? Perhaps the Skeptics can be of assistance. It is to their philosophy which we now turn.

Sextus Empiricus: The Way of Skepticism

In his *Outlines of Pyrrhonism*, Sextus Empiricus writes:

> Men of talent, who were perturbed by the contradictions in things and in doubt as to which alternatives they ought to accept, were led on to inquire what is true in things and what false, hoping by the settlement of this question to attain quietude. The main basic

---

[12]We coin the adjective "arational" in order to describe either beliefs which are not products of reason, or individuals who have not reflected upon their beliefs. We must stress the difference between "arational" and "irrational." Originally used to describe sentient beings who lacked the power to reason -- plants and animals, for instance -- the word "irrational" is often taken to mean" lacking the power to reason." Further, the term "irrational" can be used to describe beliefs that are absurd or nonsensical. On the other hand, we define "arational" as "having the power to reason, but not *using* it." Moreover, "arational" could also be used to describe *beliefs* that have not been engineered by a voluntary, rational process.

principle of the skeptic system is that of opposing to every proposition an equal proposition...

The Skeptics believed that *theory conflict* was the main cause of pain. Contrast this with Epicurus' view that arrational beliefs are the main sources of pain. This very discrepancy between the Epicureans and the Skeptics, provides an example of "conflicting theories:"

Epicureans: Pain is caused by arrational beliefs.
Skeptics: No. The main cause of pain is theory conflict.

You are already quite familiar with what it is for theories to conflict. In Chapter 1, you learned about several different philosophers, all of whom reminded us in one way or another that "our eyes are not windows," but nevertheless disagreed about the true nature of Reality. For instance:

Thales: Everything is water.
Democritus: Everything is atoms and void.
Pythagoras: Everything is number.
Parmenides: Everything is one.

The Skeptics, who were originally trying to discover the nature of Reality through philosophy and rational activity, were well aware of the many conflicting theories offered by philosophers. Moreover, the Skeptics were also well aware that they could not be certain which of these theories was the correct one. If our eyes are not windows to Reality, then how can we know whether water, atoms and void, numbers, or unity comprise Reality? The Skeptics believed that since we could not know this, we should therefore suspend judgment about the nature of things. Thus if conflicting theories are causing you pain, the Skeptics recommend that you *distance* yourself from these theories, that you suspend your judgment of them.

One gets a clear view of what the Skeptics advise by considering their recommendation in light of rational criticism. In order to eliminate the primary source of perturbedness, claim the Skeptics, one should repeatedly engage in the first step of rational criticism. In the first step of rational criticism, recall, one finds fault with a theory, and hence the truth of a theory is opposed on rational grounds. The existence of irrational magnitudes, for instance, opposed the truth of Pythagoras' theory that "everything is comprised of rational numbers." It is this sort of activity which the skeptic believes will cause us to "suspend judgment" about things, thereby leading us to a state of peace and tranquillity:

> Now that we have been saying that tranquillity follows on suspension of judgment, it will be our next task to explain how we arrive at this suspension. Speaking generally, one may say that it is the result of setting things in opposition. We oppose either appearances to appearances or objects of thought to objects of thought *or alternando*.[13]

So, according to the Skeptics, if we realize that every theory and every appearance can be opposed (i.e., can be criticized *rationally*), we will understand that it is fruitless to theorize about the nature of things. For if everything can be opposed, not only do we become perturbed, but there is also no reason for any theory to be deemed "correct." (Note that the Skeptics are *not* saying something like "To achieve peace and tranquillity, set theories against each other *and believe whichever one makes you feel better*." On the contrary, they are saying that for any theory there will be at least one opposing theory which is just as good. So, for any

---

[13]From Sextus' *Outlines of Pyrrhonism*.

theory you consider, find the opposing theory which is just as good, set the two against each other, and *don't believe either one of them*.)

In arguing that theorizing about Reality only leads to negative consequences, the Skeptics seem to be arguing against pursuing the *second* step of rational criticism. For it is the second step of rational criticism wherein one constructs a theory that is believed to be immune to criticism. The Skeptics claim that it is impossible to construct such a theory.[14]

Exercise
3.   In exercise 2 above you listed some of your beliefs which you suspect are pain-causing. Now, following the advice of the Skeptics, try to oppose these beliefs with their contraries. For example, you might oppose the belief "my love being unrequited (by so and so), means that I am undesirable" with "but there are desirable people who have their love unrequited," (for instance, Werther in Goethe's *Sorrows of a Young Werther*, or Orsino in Shakespeare's *Twelfth Night*). In other words, try to find propositions which oppose the beliefs by which you are pained.

According to the Skeptics, if you engage in this activity with *all* of your beliefs, you will eventually suspend judgment about *everything*, and achieve peace and tranquillity.[15] If you find that the recommendation of the Skeptics provides little help to the causes of your disturbances, then there is one last group of philosophers who may be of help. There are the Stoics. Let us see what they take to be the main causes of pain. And let us see what medicine they recommend.

Epictetus
Like the Epicureans, the Stoics (including Epictetus) believed that pain was caused by certain beliefs. But which beliefs? The Epicureans believed that arrational beliefs (for example, beliefs about the gods and death) are the cause of pain. The Skeptics believed that conflicting beliefs are the cause of pain. According to the Stoics, we are perturbed when we mistakenly believe that something "is our own."

> If we only realize what is and what is not our own, we can live peacefully, free of pain. Remember, then, that if you suppose things by nature slavish to be free, and what belongs to others your own, you will be hindered; you will lament; you will be disturbed; you will find fault with both the gods and men. But if you suppose that only to be your own which is your own, and what belongs to others such as it really is...you will suffer no harm.

According to the Stoics, something that is not your own is something over which you have no control. Suppose you spend hours studying for an exam. On the day of the exam you feel confident, and even eager to take it. When you see the exam, however, you realize that you

---

[14] If we take a closer look, however, the Skeptics might appear to be engaging, in their own way, in *both* steps of rational criticism if we construe them as arguing as follows:

Initial theory: It is useful to attempt to settle the question of which one of two contradictory theories (about appearances or things beyond appearances) is true. For, by settling the question of which of two contradictory theories is true, we attain quietude.

Step 1 of rational criticism: Since we can never settle the question of which of two contradictory theories about things beyond appearances is true, and since it is to painful view a plurality of contradictory theories, it is *useless* to theorize about things beyond appearances.

Step 2 of rational criticism: Suspending judgment about things is useful. For, this makes us immune to the problem of settling the question of which one of a pair of contradictory theories is true, and it is pleasant.

[15] The Danish philosopher Søren Kierkegaard (Chapter 18) recommends a quite different response to deciding between alternatives without sufficient reason: don't suspend judgment, *passionately* commit yourself to one alternative rather than the other in spite of the fact that there is no reason whatsoever for choosing either of the alternatives over the other.

are asked questions for which you did not prepare. What do you do? If you are wise, claim the Stoics, you will realize that you had no control over the exam questions. You will take the exam in peace, and do the best that you can. If you become disturbed, however, you do so because you mistakenly regarded the exam questions as "your own," or, in other words, as something of which you are in control.

The Stoics claim that we must realize what is and what is not within our power, what is and what is not our own. For only by correctly dividing the world into these two categories can we be freed from all pain. What then, is your own? Over what do you exercise control? Only yourself, only your beliefs, only your interpretations of your experiences. There is a marvelous scene in the movie *Fearless* when the main character who, while inside a plane that is plummeting to its demise, resounding with the screams of trembling passengers, takes a deep breath and says "everything is wonderful." As he calmly walks through the cabin, assuring people, touching them, comforting them during their last moments, he is in complete control of himself. He realizes that he cannot control the fate of the plane, and he crashes to the earth, in peace. Such an individual is the apotheosis of Stoic virtue. For he correctly realized that he had no control over that plane's fate.

The Stoic fully realizes that events typically cause people pain, and that many events, as we mentioned earlier, are simply not in our control. Nevertheless, the Stoics believe that we can, indeed should, confront any event, no matter how horrible, with peace. If we realized that events have their sting because of the *interpretations* we apply to them, we could engineer our beliefs in a way that would prevent us from being perturbed by any event. For if we experienced events through beliefs that correctly divide the world into what is and what is not within our power, we would live a life free of disturbance.

Exercise

4.   Once again let us return to your answers to exercise 2. According to the Stoics, beliefs cause you pain only when they are mistaken. Indeed, according to the Stoic, any time you are disturbed, you know that you are operating with corrupt beliefs. Now, with your answer to exercise 2 in mind, try to articulate for yourself what the Stoics would identify as the corruption of your belief (revealed in exercise 2). For instance, if you were disturbed by the belief "my love being unrequited (by so-and-so) means that I am undesirable," you might answer that the Stoic would say that this belief is corrupt since in having it, one fails to realize that one has no control over the actions of other people. So, articulate for yourself why the Stoic would deem your beliefs corrupt.

Concluding

You are now aware of three different theories of how to live a life free of pain. Each theory, as you have seen, both uniquely identifies the main source of pain, as well as advises how to eliminate the source. Let's summarize:

Philosopher	Primary cause of pain	Remedy
Epicurus	Beliefs about gods, death, and any other arrational beliefs about the true causes of things.	Engineer beliefs. Learn to experience pain objectively by studying philosophy (especially that of the atomists).
Sextus Empiricus	Conflicting theories	Suspend judgment by engaging in the first step of rational criticism with both theories and appearances.
Epicurus	Mistaken beliefs about what is and is not within our power.	Engineer beliefs. Become mindful of what is and what is not within our power.

Exercise

5.   You have examined your painful experiences in light of all three of these theories. Now ask yourself if you find any of these theories persuasive. Remember that each of these theories describes a method that (purportedly) enables us to the control the degree to which we are disturbed by what happens to you. Are you convinced that any of these methods will work? Have you tested them? If you have not sufficiently tested them, then do so. If after such experimentation you take these theories to fail in serving their purpose, then what do you suggest as an alternative ? As a final exercise, formulate your own view about the main cause of pain, and outline a way by which it can be eliminated.

Primary Cause of Pain   **Remedy**

Chapter 5

Catholic Philosophy

Plotinus

Three Degrees of Reality

In order to better understand Plotinus' view, it will help to review Plato's theory of forms that was discussed in Chapter 2. Recall that Plato postulated forms in order to explain the relationship between the universal and the particular. Given that there are, for example, many beautiful things -- many beautiful particulars -- the question arises as to what is common to all and only beautiful things. What makes something beautiful? Plato answered that things are beautiful because they partake in the form (or the universal) of beauty.

Plato believed that the universal -- the form -- is more real than the particular. In Plato's view, particular beautiful things are real to some extent, but not as real as the form of beauty. Plato also believed that the "form of the Good," is more real than any of the other forms. So, Plato conceived of Reality as consisting in three grades: particulars being the least real, the forms being moderately real, and form of the good being maximally real.

Plotinus, like Plato, distinguished three degrees of Reality: Soul, *nous*, and the One. Unlike Plato, however, Plotinus understood Reality as consisting not in a hierarchy of worlds or forms, but in a hierarchy of *powers* that is responsible for those worlds or forms. For instance, Soul, according to Plotinus, is the power which creates space and time -- the very manifold that makes the world of particulars possible. For Plato it is the world of particulars that is the least real. Similarly, whereas Plato believed that the world of forms was moderately real, Plotinus believed that *nous*, that was responsible for the world of forms, was moderately real. *Nous*, on Plotinus' view, is the intelligence that thinks the forms. This power and its creation (the forms) are more real than Soul and its creation (space and time, and everything in it). But, what was the most real power for Plotinus? Plato believed that the form of the Good was maximally real. Plotinus, following suit, believed that the One, which is the power responsible for the possibility of anything and everything, is maximally real.

Plato's Hierarchy	Plotinus' Hierarchy	
Form Of Good	One	
World Of Forms		Nous
World Of Particulars		Soul

But how are we to understand this notion of "degrees of Reality?" Why did Plotinus think that *nous* was more real than the Soul? Plotinus, like Plato, believed that the less a thing changes, the more real it is, and he gives the following argument for this claim: the less a thing changes, the more it possesses unity, and the more it possesses unity, the more clearly it is individuated from everything else. The more clearly something is individuated from everything else, the more precise its identity. So, since the identity of a thing is its "being," the less a thing changes the more real it is.

> For any thing of all that are called unities is so far truly one as it possesses essential Being: so that the less real has less of unity, the more real more.... The discrete bodily unities, such as a choir, are furthest from Unity proper; the continuous is somewhat nearer;

29

Soul's unity nearer still; yet even she does not communicate in the One .[16]

So, when speaking of powers, we can say that the degree to which a power is real depends upon (i) the extent to which that power is unified, and (ii) the degree to which its objects are individuated. How real is an object or a power? Determine how unified that thing is, and you can answer the question.

Let's try to see why Soul is less real than *nous* , and why *nous* is less real than the One. Now, Soul is responsible for the world of particular things (it creates space and time). But since particular things change over time, then they are not perfectly individuated. So, Soul does not govern perfectly unified objects. Since Soul is a power that governs imperfectly individuated objects, then it has a relatively low degree of Reality. On the other hand, *nous* is responsible for the world of forms. But unlike the objects of the Soul, the forms -- the objects of *nous* -- do *not* change. The forms are eternal and hence are more real than the particulars. And since the forms are eternal, *nous* is more real than the Soul. But since there are *many* forms, *nous* does not govern a perfectly individuated world. So *nous* does not enjoy the maximal degree of Reality. But the One is individuation in and of itself, the perfect individuating principle; the only of its kind, and unchanging, and alone in being self-individuating. Since the One governs only itself-- and hence the power of individuation -- it is the most Real power. For the One is not only perfectly individuated, but it also governs itself -- a perfectly individuated power.

Concluding

So, Plotinus begins with the world of particular things, notes that they are each in space and time, and postulates Soul, the generator of space and time, as their principle of individuation. He recognizes that the many objects of ordinary experience are classed into different kinds, e.g. blue things, red things, beautiful things, tables, etc. And to the question of *why* are things grouped into different kinds (e.g. into blue things or into beautiful things) he answers that all of the particulars of a given kind exemplify (or "partake in") the form for that kind (e.g. blueness or beauty). These forms are nowhere in space or time, so they obviously cannot be individuated by space and time. Therefore we cannot see them, hear them, smell them, taste them, or touch them. But, we can *think* about them. So, Plotinus figures that they are individuated by thought. He thus postulates *nous*, an intelligence that individuates the forms by thinking them. Finally, he realizes that all of the things he has just accepted the existence of (all sensible objects and all forms) are each *one* thing. And so all are, to a degree, individuated. He thus postulates the One; individuation in and of itself. Since everything is individuated, the One makes all things possible. Thus, the One is the highest principle and "beyond being."

---

[16]*Enneads*, VI.ix.1. Quotes from *Enneads* in this section are translations by E.R. Dodds in *Select Passages Illustrating Neoplatonism* (1979. Area Publishers Inc., Chicago.) By "the continuous" in the passage quoted above Plotinus is referring to elements which have the property that dividing any portion of that element will result in smaller portions of that same element. For instance, according to the chemistry of Plotinus' day, water was such an element. So, Plotinus believed that given any portion of water, we could divide it into smaller and smaller portions forever, and would always be left with smaller and smaller portions of *water*. We, on the other hand, know that a molecule of water is divisible into two hydrogen atoms and one oxygen atom, which are *not* water.

The Three Degrees of Reality

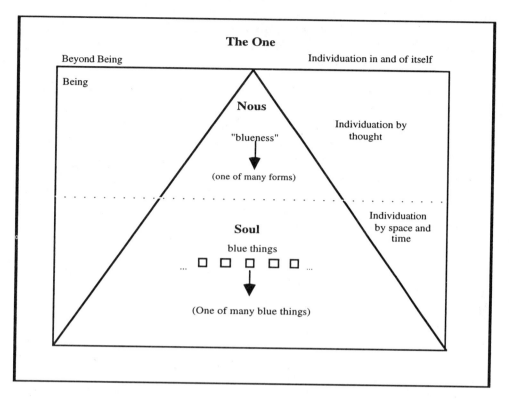

Does it follow from these considerations (of being beyond being or existence) that the One is *nothing*? Plotinus has a view about that:

> When, therefore, we consider the [principle of the] Unity of true Reals [i.e. the One], which is the Source and the Fountainhead and the Power, shall we be incredulous and suspect that this Unity is *nothing*? Certainly it is nothing of those things whereof it is the source. But it is that which exists above them all, and beyond all predicates; of which we may say neither "It is Real" nor "It is Reality" nor yet "It is Life"; yet if thou strip away even the "It exists," and grasp it so, the wonder of it shall possess thee..."[17]

Augustine

In this section we will consider three main themes raised in the Augustine selections from *Lovers of Wisdom*: self-knowledge, seeing beyond the world of inner appearances, and illumination. We will end the chapter by asking you to consider Augustine's view that will (not rationality, as Aristotle thought) is the essence of man . Your ruminations will be asked in the light of your own experience studying *Lovers of Wisdom*.

The Mind's Knowledge of Itself

In the last selection from Augustine in *Lovers of Wisdom* (Book X, Chapter 6 of *On the Trinity*) you encountered a view according to which the mind is deeply deceived about itself. In order to understand this claim, it is essential to remember that this view is about *you*. It is unlike, say, a description of the historic sites of Greece in at least the following sense: (assuming that you are now in the United States) if you were reading about Greece, you would

---

[17]*Enneads*, III.viii.10

be a long way from what you were reading about. On the other hand, in considering a theory about the mind, you are as close to what you are reading about as you can possibly get: *you are it*. The theory is about you. So, just as it would be absurd to take a trip to Greece only to sit in a hotel room and read a tour brochure about the sites, it would be absurd to read a theory of the mind without actually exploring your own. While it is fairly difficult to mistake a tour brochure for a trip through Greece, it is a very easy to mistake reading about a theory of the mind for actually observing your own mind.

In what way does Augustine think that the mind is deceived about itself? He writes that "the mind errs when it so lovingly and intimately connects itself with [images of corporeal things]...." In thinking about itself, the mind uses images which it has acquired from corporeal objects. But, on Augustine's view, the mind is a non-corporeal substance. Thus, in using these corporeal images to describe itself to itself, the mind misrepresents itself.

This is the kernel of Augustine's view on the mind's opinion of itself. Now, consider *your* mind's opinion of itself. What corporeal images has your mind "lovingly and intimately" connected with itself? In other words, what corporeal images or metaphors do you use when thinking about or describing your mind? Consider the sorts of things you think and say about your mind. For instance, consider the phrase "the back of my mind." In using such a phrase we use spatial concepts (of front and back) to describe some aspect of the mind. But, in actuality, there is no (spatial) front or back to the mind. Clearly, when we use that phrase we do not mean to refer to the back of the *head*, but to...what?

Exercises
1.　　Think of several "corporeal images" that you use to describe your mind. List five of your most uttered phrases about the mind that involve reference to physical properties. (If you get stuck, go through Augustine's selections and look for his appeals to such corporeal images in describing the mind. Try to find some that you yourself mention in your everyday life.)

Corporeal images that you associate with your own mind and the minds of others:

2.　　Now try to take the images (or metaphors) listed above and translate them into "literal" terms, free of corporeal imagery. In other words, when you say that some thought was in the back of your mind (and so on for the other phrases), what do you literally mean? (Try to avoid fashionable uses of technical terms like "subconscious" as much as possible. If you pay close attention you will find that those sorts of terms are often implicit metaphors cleverly disguised. What does "subconscious" really mean in everyday use? A small, dark "room" in your mind? Thoughts at a "lower volume" than your conscious thoughts? Ideas in the "peripheral vision" of your consciousness? These clearly are all metaphors based on images and ideas which literally apply to corporeal objects.) List your translations below, and remember that these are phrases and images that *you* use in thinking about your own mind.

Image-Free Translations:

Most likely, providing good, image-free translations proved to be difficult. Perhaps you could not translate the phrases in exercise 1 without metaphor. Augustine claims that we cannot help but think of the mind in terms of such imagery. If the only images you have are corporeal images, then you tend to think of everything like a corporeal object -- including the mind. Augustine writes that the mind is "unable to be in itself without the images of those corporeal things." What are the consequences of this view? Is the mind itself a metaphor?

Seeing Beyond the Inner world of Appearances

Kolak explains that on Augustine's view, we must see beyond the world of appearances in order to know Reality. But, if the mind cannot be alone in itself without these corporeal images (without "the inner world of appearances"), what can we do to see beyond them?

Well, what is it that allows Augustine to discover these things about the mind? At the least, he must recognize that these corporeal images which we apply to the mind *are images*. That is, he must see the images *as* images. To understand this clearly, we will distinguish "seeing" from "seeing *as*" using the picture below.[18] Stare at the picture and ask yourself what it is a picture *of*. Then stare at it even longer. What happens?

Does the image suddenly changes from a picture of a duck to a picture of a rabbit, or vice versa? At one moment you should see a picture of a duck. At another moment you should see a picture of a rabbit. In both cases one is *seeing* the same image, but in the first case one is seeing it *as* a duck, and in the second case one is seeing it *as* a rabbit.

Augustine's insight that the mind's opinion of itself is deceitful could not have occurred to him unless he had first seen the corporeal images, which the mind connects to itself, *as corporeal images*. In other words, to use the example of "the back of my mind," in order to understand that this phrase is derived from corporeal objects, one must first realize that "back" and "front" are properties of corporeal objects. Thus, given his view that the mind is *not* corporeal, once Augustine notices that the mind is describing itself to itself using corporeal metaphors, he concludes that the mind is deceiving itself. Had he failed to see the corporeal images as images, he would never have known that the mind connects these images to itself, and so he never would have had the insight that the mind is deceived about itself.

So, with the help of the duck/rabbit picture above, we become acquainted with the distinction between seeing and seeing as; we see a single image, at one time, as a duck and, at another, as a rabbit. Let's apply our understanding of this distinction to our awareness of our own minds. Notice the difference between the sense you had of the phrase "the back of my mind" before we discussed it above (or before you thought of it yourself in a similar way), and the sense you have of that phrase after noting that it is at best metaphorical. You now grasp the mind in terms of corporeal pictures, in terms of "the back of the mind," and the others terms you listed above. You grasp the mind as having this or that corporeal property. But these are pictures derived from physical objects.

Even the phrase "*my* mind" is very unclear. Does your mind *belong* to you? If so, in what sense? Like an article of clothing? Does your mind belong to you because only you can "see inside it"?[19] Similarly, common phrases like "part of me wants this but another part of me wants that," and many others that we often use in talking about our minds, are metaphorical. The question to ask yourself at this point is this: is it possible to think about the mind in terms which are not metaphorical, to perceive the mind as it is in itself independently of this or that interpretation of it, to grasp it directly?[20]

---

[18]This picture can be found in Wittgenstein's *Philosophical Investigations*.

[19]In fact, in the next chapter we will see that the Islamic philosopher Averroes argued that there is only one mind in the universe.

[20]Plotinus' thought it was possible. His description of *nous* ("the divine intellect") is a description of such a direct awareness of the mind.

Illumination

As you read in Kolak's discussion of Augustine, Augustine held that "No amount of study will help [one to attain knowledge of God], no amount of learning, not even prayer will make any difference whatsoever." Such illumination must come of itself from God and is not in the control of the mind. In order to get a clearer sense of what this view is about, let's think of some examples of illumination which are a bit more ordinary and familiar to us, and think about the sense in which these are not in the control of the mind (or at least the "conscious" mind).

Do you think that you are in control of creative insights? Do you think that creative insights are willed? If you do not, then you can start to grasp what Augustine meant by "illumination." Indeed, many mathematicians, artists, scientists etc. suggest, in one way or another, that creative insights often come only when they have *stopped* working on the problem, as if out of nowhere. For instance, the mathematician Henri Poincaré writes:

> The incidents of [a geological excursion] made me forget my mathematical work. Having reached Countenances, we entered an omnibus to go some place or other. At the moment when I put my foot on the step the idea came to me, without anything in my former thoughts seeming to have paved the way for it, that the transformations I had used to define the Fuchsian functions were identical to those of non-Euclidean geometry.[21]

Poincaré indeed suggests that his insight into the nature of Fuchsian functions seemed to have come 'out of nowhere.' What does this show? At least that, in many cases, creative insights are not controlled by the conscious mind. Augustine, in denying that any such insight is the product of the conscious mind, would explain such extraordinary events with divine illumination. Such inspiration is a result of God's divine grace. For Augustine, revelation (i.e., knowledge of God) is acquired in much the same way.

Exercise

3. Augustine believed that no amount of rational argument can change one's beliefs. Only a change in one's will can affect a change in beliefs. Consider your own experience in reading *Lovers of Wisdom*. Would you say that your own beliefs have changed as a result of reading *Lovers of Wisdom*? If your beliefs have changed, what do you think *made* them change; the *rational arguments*, or a *desire* to change your beliefs, to think about things differently, etc.? If your beliefs haven't changed, why didn't they; the arguments were not good enough, or you desire to hold on to your beliefs?

---

[21]Jacques Hadamard, *The Psychology of Invention in the Mathematical Field* (Princeton, 1945) p. 13.

Chapter 6

The Spanish-Islamic Influence

Averroes

The Most Difficult of All Truths

In Chapter 6 of *Lovers of Wisdom*, Kolak writes that Averroes took the most difficult of all truths to be that "the active part of the mind of each human being is not a distinct and separately existing individual, but is the same, numerically identical unity." In this chapter we will proceed from the simplest toward the most difficult of truths by ascending, as it were, from the book you are now reading, through your mind, and into the active intellect. Among the simplest of truths is this: you are now reading a book. We will move from this truth toward Averroes' most difficult of truths by understanding his interpretation of three Aristotelian concepts:

> (i) Particulars and Universals
> (ii) Primary Substance
>   (a) Your book
>   (b) Your mind
> (iii) The Passive and Active Intellects

Particulars and Universals

In previous chapters, you were introduced to the distinction between singular and general terms, and to the corresponding distinction between particulars (say, the particular book you are now reading) and forms or "universals" (say, "bookhood"). Plato and Aristotle, as you know, both used the term "form," but used it in different senses. The difference between their uses of this term was discussed in Chapter 3. The Platonic term for the form associated with books, for instance, is "bookhood." "Bookhood" is eternal and exists in the realm of the "really real," independently of the existence of any books. On Aristotle's view, however, the form associated with books is dependent on the existence of particular books and on minds which "abstract" the form from these particulars by coming to understand what it is for something to be a book. For this reason the Aristotelian form associated with books is called "the intelligible form of what it is to be a book" (or "what it is to be a book" for short).[22] To keep these different uses of "form" clear, in this chapter we will call Platonic forms "universals." So, in this chapter, "form" will always be used in the Aristotelian sense, unless otherwise noted.

Throughout this chapter we will take the book that you are now reading, on the one hand, and "bookhood," on the other, as respective examples of a particular and a universal. These examples will serve to illustrate our points as we elucidate Averroes' interpretation of Aristotle. In order to move from the particular book before you to the active intellect, let's

---

[22]Another way to think of this form in the Aristotelian sense is to think of it as what causes something to be a book rather than, say, a pencil. Aristotle distinguishes four types of causes: (i) the *formal* cause ("what it is to be" a such and such), (ii) the *material* cause ("that out of which" some object is made), (iii) the *efficient* cause ("that by which" some object or event is the way it is), and (iv) the *final* cause ("that for the sake of which" some object is made or some event happens). Hence, when referring to Aristotle's concept of the form associated with books we say "what it is to be a book," instead of "bookhood."

briefly recall Aristotle's concept of *primary substance* by focusing on the two examples of primary substance closest at hand -- your book and your mind.

Primary Substance

We first presented Aristotle's view of primary substance in Chapter 3. Recall from that chapter that every primary substance consists of two aspects; matter and form:

> Now there is one class of existent things which we call substance, including under the term, firstly, matter, which in itself is not this or that; secondly, shape or form, in virtue of which the term this or that is at once applied; thirdly, the whole made up of matter and form.

Let's make this view intelligible to ourselves by focusing on our two examples of primary substance; your book on the one hand, and your mind on the other.
(a) Your Book

The particular book you are reading, according to Aristotle's metaphysics, is an individual primary substance composed of matter and form.

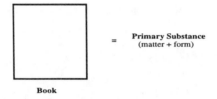

Book

= **Primary Substance**
(matter + form)

This does *not* mean that it is composed of a *particular* lump of matter (paper, ink, etc.) and the *universal* (Platonic form) of bookhood. As Averroes points out in his commentary to *Text 5*, Aristotle holds that, in the case of non-mental (or non-thinking) primary substances, each particular has its own particular form. Thus, Averroes writes "...prime matter [that is, the material component of non-mental primary substances, like your book] receives differentiated, that is, individual and particular forms..." So, the book you are now reading has its own, individual formal component that is distinct from the formal component of any other object. Thus, the formal component of your book is not a Platonic universal . On Plato's view particular books all partake in the same universal (or form) of bookhood. According to Aristotle, however, each particular book has its own form.

This is brought out in the quote from Aristotle above when he states that the *matter* "is not this or that," e.g. it is not any particular kind of thing (say, a book as opposed to a pencil), nor is it any particular object (say, one book rather than another book). The *form*, on the other hand, is "[that] in virtue of which the term this or that is at once applied." To apply the term "this" or "that," in this context, means the matter has become a particular *kind* of object (e.g. a book), and has become a *particular* object of that kind (e.g. the very book you are now reading and no other). The book you are now reading is a different object than the book that your classmate owns. This object is not that object. They are both books, and are both books with the same title, but because they each have their own individual forms, they are not the same object (primary substance).

So, the form that individuates the book you are now reading from every other object is and must be particular to the very book you are now reading and nothing else. It is in virtue of the particularity of the form in question that the book in question is individuated from everything else. This form is therefore not "common to all and only books," for it is common to nothing but a single book. And so, it is clearly not the Platonic universal "bookhood." Bookhood, says Aristotle, is a universal and intelligible form, "abstracted" by the mind from particular books. Bookhood is not the form which, together with the matter, makes up your book. Recalling the distinction between primary and secondary substance discussed in Chapter 3, "bookhood" is a secondary substance, whereas the Aristotelian form that is particular to your book is, in conjunction with the matter, a primary substance. Think of secondary substances as abstract entities, and think of primary substances as concrete entities. "Bookhood" is an abstraction, a secondary substance. Your book, on the other hand, is a concrete entity, a primary substance. The form of *your* book is referred to as a *material* or *substantial form*.[23]

(b) Your Mind

Just like the book you are reading, your mind also, on Aristotle's view, is a primary substance made up of matter and form.

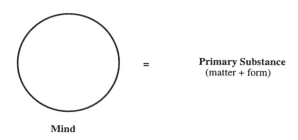

As in the case of unthinking objects, like your book, to say that the mind is made up of matter and form does *not* mean that your mind is composed of a *particular* "cloud of mental stuff" and the Platonic *universal* of mindhood. Again, the matter "is not this or that," and the form is "[that] in virtue of which the term this or that is applied."

The Passive and Active Intellects

Aristotle refers to the material aspect of mind as the *passive intellect*, and refers to the formal aspect of mind as the *active intellect*.. But why does Aristotle call these "passive" and "active" intellects? In his commentary to *Text 4*, Averroes explains:

> For, insofar as the intelligibles move [the intellect] it is passive, but insofar as they are moved by it, it is active. For this reason Aristotle states subsequently that it is necessary to posit in the rational soul the following distinct [powers], namely an active power and a passive power.

What is Averroes saying? What is the "movement" that he is referring to? Consider again our example of a particular (the book you are now reading) and a Platonic universal (the intelligible form of "bookhood"). What is it for the *intelligible form* of "bookhood" to "move" the *intellect*? Roughly speaking, when you look at this book your eyes and brain produce a visual perception of a particular book. In addition, you *recognize that it is a book*.[24] (To use terms from Chapter 5, you see the book and see it *as* a book.) As Kolak points out, neither of these events (your perception or your recognition of the book) are the result of a conscious thought process. "...[T]o represent objects to itself the mind does not consciously do anything." So, the instantaneous recognition that it is *a book* that you perceive is what Aristotle is calling a case of the intelligible form of what it is to be a book "moving" the intellect. This aspect of the mind, the capacity for an instantaneous recognition that something before you is a such-and-such, is the *passive intellect*.[25]

---

[23]Averroes uses the term "material form," while, for instance, Leibniz uses the term "substantial form."

[24]Of course, the perception of the book and the recognition that it is a *book* that you are seeing occur basically at the same time (now that you are an expert at recognizing books). Nonetheless, you can imagine these two events in isolation, for instance when a child perceives a book before learning how to recognize books. This will be discussed in more detail in Chapter 16.

[25]The *perception* is generated by the senses. The passive intellect is connected with the *recognition* that you are perceiving a such-and-such, say a book. This recognition is the movement of the passive intellect by a form.

Now we must ask what it is for the *intellect* to "move" the *intelligible form* of "bookhood." The intellect moves this intelligible form by *thinking of* bookhood. One can perform this act partially. That is, one can fall short of the mark by thinking that, say, to be a book is simply to have pages. This is an inadequate definition of bookhood. Certainly it is partly right, but more information is required to fully capture the nature of bookhood. One is not thinking of what it is to be a book unless one has captured all (and only) the information which correctly describes what it is to be a book. Thus, the closer one comes to fully comprehending what it is to be a book, the more one "moves" the intelligible form of bookhood. In the act of thinking of what it is to be a book, the intellect moves the intelligible form of bookhood. The aspect of the mind which performs this act is the *active intellect.*[26]

Hopefully, after the discussion of Augustine's view of corporeal images and the mind's false opinion of itself (in Chapter 5), you will be cautious enough not to confuse movement of the intellect with the movement of objects through space. In other words, if the above quote leads you to imagine that the mind sometimes pushes forms around and sometimes gets pushed around by them, like a billiard ball on a crowded table, you will have been misled into thinking of the mind and the intelligible forms as if they were corporeal objects. They are not. This image is helpful, but only metaphorical. "Movement" in the above discussion is an analogy for recognition and thought. Strictly speaking, the movement that is characteristic of intelligible forms is a cognitive, indeed an intellectual, movement. And when we remember that cognition is aspatial, we become mindful that the movement of which Averroes speaks is not a spatial, not a corporal, movement.

To summarize, you effortlessly recognize a book when you see one. And yet, as Socrates' method of inquiry shows us, you cannot express what it is to be a book nearly as easily. How can this be? How can you recognize a book when you see one, and yet not know what it is for something to be a book? Aristotle answer is that there are different intellectual faculties that are responsible for these mental activities: the recognition that some particular thing before you is a book takes place through the passive intellect, while the understanding of what it is to be a book takes place through the active intellect.

Exercise

Recall *Text 5:*

> And thus [the material intellect] has no other nature but that which is possible. Therefore that [part] of the soul which is called intellect (and I call intellect that part by means of which we distinguish and think) is not something existing in actuality before it thinks.

In what way is the quotation from Hasan of Basra (at the beginning of this chapter) relevant to the theory of the mind we have just examined (as emphasized in *Text 5*)?

Averroes sometimes calls these forms "imaginative forms." He defines them as "intelligible forms in potentiality." See Averroes' commentary to *Text 4.*

[26]Averroes sometimes calls the intelligible forms that are moved by the active intellect "speculative intelligibles." In a part of his commentary not included in *Lovers of Wisdom* he writes "...the intelligibles in actuality, that is the speculative intelligibles, are generable according to the object through which they are true, that is according to the imaginative forms."

Chapter 7

The Medievals

The positions of Aquinas, Duns Scotus, and Ockham, that were presented in Chapter 7 of *Lovers of Wisdom*, are in some respects quite difficult. Understanding *what* they were trying to show is often impossible without understanding *how* they were trying to show it. One understands how someone shows their position, when one understands the structure and content of their *arguments*. So, we devote this chapter to explaining (i) how to make explicit the structure of an argument, and (ii) how to evaluate an argument.[27] After learning these skills, you will be better able to understand not only the complex material in Chapter 7 and in later chapters of *Lovers of Wisdom*, but also the positions argued for in virtually any field. For, arguments are by no means peculiar to philosophy. Quite the contrary; any form of discourse that involves asserting the truth of certain statements, on the one hand, and, on the other, giving reasons for why one should believe these assertions, involves argumentation.

The Function and Structure of Arguments

It is useful to think of an argument as a way of making explicit one's *reasons* for believing a certain proposition. Suppose, for example, that you believe that God exists. If you are asked why you believe that God exists, you may respond by saying, "because something must have created the universe."[28] In making this claim, you are making explicit your reason for maintaining a certain belief, and hence are advancing an argument. We call the statements given as reasons for believing some proposition *premises*. In the example above, only one reason is given in support of the statement "God exists," and hence the above argument has only one premise. Arguments, however, can have many premises. We will see that the arguments of Aquinas, for instance, always involve more than one premise.

In our example, the premise "something must have created the universe," is used to support the statement "God exists." The latter statement is the *conclusion* of the argument. Just as an argument may contain more than one premise, arguments may likewise contain more than one conclusion. Arguments that have multiple conclusions are called *complex arguments*, and arguments that have only one conclusion are called *simple arguments*. Since the above argument contains only one conclusion, it is a simple argument. The structure of such an argument is usually represented by drawing a horizontal line between the premise(s) and the conclusion. Thus:

(1) Something must have created the universe.

----

(2) God exists.

---

[27]There is a distinction between *deductive* and *inductive* arguments. In a deductively valid argument, the truth of the premises *guarantees* the truth of the conclusion. In an inductively strong argument, on the other hand, the truth of the premises makes highly probable the truth of the conclusion. In this chapter, we limit our discussion to deductive arguments.

[28]Incidentally, as it stands this is not a very good argument. One can always ask the further question, "But what created God?" If you claim that God is eternal, and therefore needs no creator, you will have to answer some difficult questions before you have a strong argument, for instance why can't the universe be eternal and exist without a creator?

We can also represent the structure of a *complex* argument in this way. As an example, let's use Zeno's paradox. Recall Zeno's argument for the impossibility of motion (from Chapter 1):

(1) If a thing is to move, then it must move from one point (a) to another point (b).

(2) Between any two points there are an infinite number of points.
----
(3) Therefore, if a thing is to move, then it must traverse an infinite number of points.
(4) It is impossible to traverse an infinite number of points.
----
(5) Therefore, motion is impossible.

Note that sentence (3) serves as both the conclusion of sentences (1) and (2), *and* as a premise that, with sentence (4), entails the main conclusion sentence (5).

Indicators of Argument Structure

Well, there are often key terms that indicate whether a sentence is either functioning as a premise or as conclusion, and thereby disclose the structure of the argument. For instance, in the argument, "God exists because something must have created the universe," the word "because" signals that "something must have created the universe" is the *premise*: And so, as above, the argument-structure is made explicit as follows:

(1) Something must have created the universe.
----
(2) God exists

Similarly, in the argument "There is life, therefore God exists," the word "therefore" signals that "God exists" is the *conclusion*:

(1) There is life.
----
(2) God exists.

We call terms that signal premises *premise indicator terms*, and terms that signal conclusions *conclusion indicator terms*. A partial list of both types of indicator terms is provided below.

Common premise indicator terms	Common conclusion indicator terms
because	therefore
for	so
since	consequently
firstly	it follows that
assuming	proves that
but	thus

When trying to extract the structure of an argument from ordinary language, it is good practice to first find and circle the indicator terms. (Sometimes, however, an argument will not have any of these terms. In this case one can ask, "what is the point of this passage? what is it asking me to believe?" These questions can help bring out the conclusions. And one can ask "on what basis am I supposed to believe the conclusions of the passage?" This latter question can help make the premises explicit.) After circling the indicator terms, number each of the statements, and then try to find the main conclusion of the argument. Then, after paraphrasing each statement so that redundancy is eliminated, order the paraphrased statements in a way which seems to best capture the structure of the argument.

Representing Argument Structure

(i) **circle** indicator terms
(ii) **number** each statement
(iii) **find** main conclusion
(iv) **paraphrase** so that redundancy is eliminated and clarity is enhanced
(v) **order** paraphrased statements

Let's illustrate each of these:

> Since my parents told me so, and because my parents tell the truth, it is clear that God exists.

There are two premise indicator terms and one conclusion indicator term (one of them is not on the above list). **Circle** them. There are a total of three statements implicit in this sentence, only one of which is the conclusion. After making them explicit and **paraphrasing** (i.e., eliminating redundancy and enhancing clarity), we are left with:

> God exists. **[Conclusion]**
> My parents told me that God exists.
> My parents always tell the truth.

After **ordering** these statements (the conclusion should appear as the last statement, not as the first) the *structure* of the argument is made explicit:

> (1) My parents always tell the truth.
> (2) My parents told me that God exists.
> ---
> (3) God exists

Exercise

1.   Before trying these skills on the arguments of Aquinas, try to represent the logical structure of the following arguments:

> (i) The dog is man's best friend, so the cat must be man's enemy. After all, dogs and cats fight.
>
> (ii) His power is infinite; whatever he wills is executed; but neither man nor any animal is happy; therefore, he does not will their happiness.
>
> (iii) Clearly God does not exist. For an all good God would not allow evil in the world. And there is evil.

When you first read Aquinas' arguments for the existence of God, you probably found them somewhat difficult. We will go through the first one with you, and then you are on your own. When you start converting the arguments for yourself, you should know that there might be times when it is difficult to even see an argument. If this is the case, *at least start somewhere.* You'll accomplish more than you may think.

Look at *"The First Way."* Note how your translator divided this argument into 8 "pieces." This tells us very little about the structure of the argument. Look at pieces (2) and (7), for instance. They both say:

Everything which is moved by something is moved by something else.

Since premise (2) is synonymous with premise (7), one of them will be eliminated when we paraphrase the argument. So again, the fact that your translator decided to carve up this argument into 8 pieces, says little about its structure.

First we should find all the indicator terms. There are many of these. In fact, each piece has at least one indicator term. Try to find the rest of the indicator terms, and circle them. Next, we need to number the statements. In doing so, it should become more clear that the fact that the passage is divided into 8 pieces has very little to do with the structure of the argument. For instance, look at piece (4). Within this one piece, we are given the following argument:

4.2. To cause movement is nothing else than to bring something
from potentiality to actuality.

4.3. A thing cannot be brought from potentiality to actuality except
by something which exists in actuality....

4.1. A thing causes movement insofar as it is in actuality.

Thus, when you are numbering the statements in Aquinas' argument, remember that within each of the eight "pieces," there may be one or more arguments.

Exercise
1.   Try now to number each of the statements in Aquinas' argument.

For our third step, the main conclusion needs to be identified. Aquinas states this both at the beginning and at the end of his argument. After **finding** the conclusion, **order** the premises in a way that best represents the structure of the argument. Do not forget to eliminate redundancy.

Here is how we think the structure of Aquinas' first argument is best represented:

(1) Motion exists.

(3) Nothing is in motion except insofar as it is in potentiality in relation to that towards which is in motion.

(4) A thing causes movement insofar as it is in actuality.[29]

(6) A thing cannot be brought from potentiality to actuality except by something which exists in actuality.
----
(7) It is not possible that the same thing should be at the same time in actuality and potentiality in relation to the same thing.[30]

---

[29]This statement is supported by statement **5**: "To cause movement is nothing else than..."
[30]This statement is supported by statement **8**: "What is hot in actuality cannot.."

(9) It is not possible that in relation to the same thing and in the same way, anything should both cause movement and be caused.

----

(10) Everything that is in motion must be moved by another.

----

(11) If the thing which causes motion is in motion, it must be moved by another.

(12) We cannot proceed to an infinity.[31]

----

(14) It is necessary to stop at a first mover.

----

(15) [A first mover exists and] this we call God.

Exercise

2.   Now try to repeat these steps with Aquinas' *second* argument (fortunately, it is much briefer than his first argument). Remember the five steps:

(i) **circle** indicator terms
(ii) **number** each statement
(iii) **find** main conclusion
(iv) **paraphrase** so that redundancy is eliminated and clarity is enhanced.
(v) **order** paraphrased statements

Evaluating an Argument

We now are ready to *evaluate* such arguments. How can we tell if Aquinas' arguments are good ones? What if we are suspicious of his arguments and want to raise criticisms -- how would we do so? Usually, most arguments are criticized by either showing (i) that the argument is *invalid*, and/or (ii) that one or more of the premises is false. Let us briefly describe how to criticize arguments in both of these ways.

Recall our argument:

If the dog is man's best friend, then the cat must be man's enemy, since dogs and cats fight.

We can represent this simple argument as:

1. Dogs and cats fight.
2. The dog is man's best friend.

----

3. The cat is man's enemy.

In order to see whether this argument is invalid, ask yourself, "*does the conclusion follow from the premises?*" One exercise that will help you to answer this question, is to see if you can conceive of a single situation in which the premises are true, and the conclusion is false. If you *can* imagine such a situation, the argument is *invalid*; and if you *cannot* imagine such a situation, then it may be that the argument is *valid*. Indeed, it is quite easy to imagine a situation in which both (i) the above premises are *true* and (ii) the conclusion is *false*. There is nothing inconsistent in thinking as much. Therefore, this argument is invalid. In an invalid argument, the relationship between the premises and conclusion is *loose* -- it is possible to have true premises with a false conclusion. In a valid argument, on the other hand, the truth of the premises *guarantees* the truth of the conclusion. An example of such an argument is:

---

[31]This statement is supported by statement **13**: "There would be no first mover..."

(1) If it is raining, the ground is wet.
(2) It is raining.
----
(3) The ground is wet.

Try to imagine a situation in which the premises are true and the conclusion is false (at the same time). With this argument, it is impossible to imagine such a situation, and hence this argument is valid. Look at Aquinas' arguments, and judge for yourself whether the conclusions follows from the premises.

We mentioned above that, one may also criticize an argument by showing that at least one of its premises is false. In order to do this, look at each premise, and ask "is it true?" If it is not, then you have raised a criticism against the argument. Although this procedure is relatively straightforward,[32] it is nonetheless crucial that you are mindful of the difference between the validity of an argument, on the one hand, and the truth of its premises, on the other. For many beginning students in philosophy tend to conflate these two notions.

The Relationship Between Validity and Truth

In order to see that the validity of an argument has very little to do with the truth of the premises, consider the following (valid) argument in which there is at least one false premise:

(1) If snow is white, then dogs can fly.
(2) Snow is white.
----
(3) Dogs can fly.

Premise 1 is obviously *false*. Does this mean that the argument is invalid? *No*. Validity, remember, concerns the *relationship* between the *premises and the conclusion* of an argument. Whether a statement is true, on the other hand, concerns the relationship between *a proposition and the world*. We say that an argument is valid, *if* the truth of the conclusion is guaranteed by the truth of the premises, but this is very different from saying *that* the premises are true. Notice that in the above argument, the truth of the conclusion is guaranteed by the truth of the premises. For *if* the premises are true, then the conclusion must be true. The argument, then, is valid -- *even though it does not have all true premises*.

The upshot of all of this is that, one's understanding of an argument does not stop after its structure has been made explicit. For one must sharpen one's focus, zoom in on the structure, first looking at the relationship between the premises and the conclusion, and then looking at the relationship between the statements involved and the world. If you therefore want to know whether Aquinas' (or any) arguments are good, you can do the following three things:

(i) represent the logical structure of the argument,

(ii) check to see if the argument is valid (ask do the premises necessitate the conclusion?),

(iii) check to see if the premises are true.

Ockham's Razor

In Chapter 7 of *Lovers of Wisdom*, Kolak briefly discusses "Ockham's Razor," the principle that demands that we refrain from multiplying entities beyond necessity. This

----

[32]Sometimes ambiguity will make it difficult to determine whether a sentence is true or false.

principle states, in other words, that a theory that commits us to the existence of a multitude of objects -- spiritual beings, abstract objects as well as physical objects, for instance -- is not to be accepted over a theory that can explain the same facts while committing us to fewer objects. In short, when attempting to predict and explain certain things, the fewer things you use, the better. So, if there are two competing theories that predict and explain the same things, we should prefer the one that does so with the least amount of objects.

But why? Why should we endorse Ockham's Razor? What's so virtuous about a theory that commits one to fewer kinds of things? Is the simpler theory to be preferred because simplicity is a guide to truth? Surely not! It is possible, after all, that the ontologically simplest theory is just plain wrong. Suppose, for example, that Jones was abducted by time-traveling aliens from the planet Mongo. The curious disappearance of Jones might be most economically explained by positing Jones' disgruntlement with his present state of life and need for escape. Maybe a note was even found on his desk stating as much. The simplicity and "ontological parsimony" of the latter theory does not make it true, however. *Truth need not cooperate with our ability to make a long story short!* But now, a philosopher is much more interested in truth than in simplicity. A philosopher seeks to understand the way the world is, even if considerations of simplicity fall by the wayside. But then the question remains. Why should we embrace the Ockhamian imperative?

Ockham's Razor is to be applied when more than one theory consistently explains the observable phenomena. So, in one sense it is arbitrary which theory we endorse. But it is not out of pure laziness that Ockham suggests we pick the simpler theory. It is out of pure love of wisdom and responsibility toward unearthing the truth.

Given any theory that consistently explains some phenomena, there is an indeterminate (maybe infinite) number of ontologically more complex theories that are able to consistently explain the phenomena. To see this, consider some already established theory, say, molecular theory. Now replace every occurrence of the term 'oxygen atom' with 'angel' and replace every occurrence of the term 'hydrogen atom' with 'devil,' leaving everything all else the same. The theory then tells us that angels and devils are the building blocks of water, H_2O. According to this new theory, call it "molecular theory*," it is the properties of spiritual beings that explain why water behaves the way that it does, e.g. why it freezes, why it evaporates, why it boils, etc. We could replace explanations involving electrons orbiting the nuclei in hydrogen and oxygen atoms with explanations involving a number of flaps per set of wings, and we could substitute talk of positive and negative charge with that of reflections of eternal goodness and evil. On this new theory, maybe, water freezes when the devils descend into hell, water evaporates when the angles fly up to heaven , and water boils when the angles and devils battle to control water, the element most essential to life. Of course, we could go on to fill the molecular world with even more furniture (like a fifth dimension, eternal chi, monsters, ether, gods, numbers, etc.). The new over-populated theory we could call 'molecular theory**'.

But on what basis can we claim that molecular theory* and molecular theory** are illegitimate theories? Why do we think that molecular theory *simpliciter* is to be preferred over molecular theory* and molecular theory**? It seems that we not only need some principled way of deeming these to be illegitimate theories, but also some reliable method for determining which theory (out of a competitive multitude) should be deemed "true." Ockham's Razor is this method. It precludes an infinite number of arbitrary, improbable theories from being accepted in favor of (in most cases) one, probable theory. Ockham's Razor is reliable; it tends to track the truth.

Chapter 8

The Renaissance

Nicholas of Cusa

In this chapter we view the work of Nicholas of Cusa through a single word: "contraction." He claims that "...all things are contracted in order to form each creature." In considering what he means by this we will (i) clarify Cusa's main claim that "everything is everything," (ii) gain a clearer understanding of predicates and relations (important concepts throughout *Lovers of Wisdom*), (iii) foreshadow the views of Leibniz (Chapter 12) and Hegel (Chapter 17), and (iv) make an important point about the process of rational criticism. We will explore the concept of contraction by constructing a miniature universe, and by showing how objects within this universe can be formed by contraction.[33]

Objects, Predicates, and Relations

First let's discuss objects, predicates, and relations. In Chapter 2 you learned about predicates, for instance "___ is a book." Predicates are linguistic items that represent properties, (e.g., the property of being a book). We say that predicates are true or false of objects, depending on whether the object in question has or exemplifies the property represented by the predicate. So, the predicate "___ is a book" is, as one would expect, true of all and only books since all and only books have the property represented by that predicate. And the predicate "___ is a book" is, for example, false of all apples since no apples are books.

Predicates are sometimes thought of as one-place relations. "Place," in this context, refers to a place for a name or description of something. Consider the following sentences:

(i) *Lovers of Wisdom* is a book.
(ii) What you are now reading is a book.

These two sentences are formed by filling in the blank in "___ is a book." In case (i) the blank is filled with a name, and in case (ii) the blank is filled with a description. There are also two-place relations, for example "___ is taller than ___." In order to form a statement from such linguistic entities we need two names or descriptions (or one of each) to fill in the blanks, as in

(iii) The Sears Tower is taller than the Empire State Building.

So, predicates are true of individual objects (e.g. the book you are reading), and two-place relations are true of ordered pairs of objects (e.g. <the Sears Tower, the Empire State Building>).[34] There are also three-, four-, five-place relations, and so on, that are respectively

---

[33]The first half of this treatment of Cusa's views may seem a bit dry, especially in comparison to the mysticism of Cusa's assertions. However, by approaching Cusa in this way we will be able to interpret his unfamiliar mysticism in terms of unambiguous concepts. We are not de-mystifying Cusa. Rather, we are *re*-mystifying the familiar (the world of our everyday experience) by putting Cusa's mystical insights into clear, ordinary terms.

[34]Note that, in general, two-place relations are true of *ordered* pairs of objects, and not simply of pairs of objects. For, some two-place relations, such as "___ is taller than ___", are such that if you switch the places of the names (or descriptions) which fill in the blanks, you turn a true sentence into a false one. So, the relation will be true of the pair taken in one order, but not in the other. For instance, the two-place relation "___ is taller than ___" is true of the ordered pair <the Sears Tower, the Empire State Building>, but is not true of the ordered pair <the

true of ordered triples, ordered quadruples, ordered quintuples, etc. Suppose we wanted to make a general claim about relations of any degree (e.g., three, four, five, etc., place relations), how would we do so? When speaking of relations in general, we use the expression "n-place relation." Think of "n" as ranging over numbers. So when we speak of an n-place relation, we are speaking of *any* relation that has a finite number of places. Think of an n-place relation as being an "any place" relation.

Now there is a way of transforming, indeed of "squeezing," relations into a predicates. In other words, we can transform an n-place relation into a one-place relation (a predicate) by filling in n-1 of its blanks. Suppose we have a two place relation (and hence n=2), say, "___ is taller than ___." How do we transform this relation into a predicate? Simply fill in n-1 of its blanks. Now since, in our case, n=2, then we are going to fill in 2-1 blanks. So, we are going to fill in one blank. With what? With a name or description. So lets do so by filling in one of the blanks with the definite description: "the Empire State Building." See how we have transformed a two place relation into a predicate?

| Two-place relation | "___ is taller than ___." |
| One-place relation (predicate) | "___ is taller than the Empire State Building." |

"___ is taller than the Empire State Building," is a predicate that is true of some individual objects (e.g. the Sears Tower), and false of others (e.g. the Leaning Tower of Pisa). But note that "___ is taller than the Empire State Building," is unlike the predicates "___ is a book," "___ is 100ft. tall," etc. For the latter predicates are not formed from relations. Let's call predicates like "___ is taller than the Empire State Building" *relational predicates*. Relational predicates, as we will see below, are the key to Cusa's concept of "contraction." So, we will now make this concept explicit, in order to better understand Cusa's view that each thing in the universe is formed by the contraction of all. This will enable us to understand his claim that "everything is everything."

Contraction

We begin by creating a miniature universe **u**, and a miniature language L, and by forming the objects in this universe by "contraction." To keep things simple, **u** will consist of five objects (including itself), and L will have five names, and a few predicates and relations. (As you will see, we will have to pay for this simplicity later). Within the context of the example we will give definitions for (i) what it is to form (the concept of) an object, (ii) what it means for one object to be "in" another, and (iii) what it is for all to be in all and each in each.

We should mention that in the example below we are, strictly speaking, forming *the concept* of an object (in the language L). Cusa, on the other hand, was concerned with the formation of the objects ("creatures") themselves. Since the conceptual parallel to Cusa's view is the easiest to illustrate, we have chosen to discuss his view in these terms.

Our miniature universe **u** and our language L, are represented below.

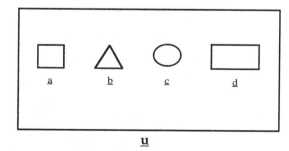

L: Names ('a', 'b', 'c', 'd', 'u'), predicates (P1-P4), and relations (R1-R3).

Empire State Building, the Sears Tower> since (iii) is true and "The Empire State Building is taller than the Sears Tower" is false.

Names:	'a', 'b', 'c', 'd', 'u'

Predicates:
P_1=___ is a square.
P_2=___ is a circle.
P_3=___ is a triangle.
P_4=___ is a rectangle.

Relations:
R_1=___ is to the left of ___ .
R_2=___ is to the right of ___ .
R_3=___ has more sides than ___ .

So, we have our universe and our language. Now, let's define what it means to *form* (the concept of) the objects within our miniature universe.

DEFINITION I: *TO form (the concept of) x (in L)* = To **list** all that can truly be said of x in **L**.

Let's illustrate this by forming the concept of a, the square. First we ask which predicates are true of a. To answer this we must (1) pull the name 'a' out of the list of names of objects and use it to fill in the blank of each predicate, and (2) ask which of the resulting statements are true:

$P_1(a)$ = a is a square.	**True**
$P_2(a)$ = a is a circle.	**False**
$P_3(a)$ = a is a triangle.	**False**
$P_4(a)$ = a is a rectangle.	**True**

But, this alone does not say *all* there is to say about a (in L). In order to form a we still need to know its relations to the other objects in the universe (u). We find this out by (3) turning our relations into relational predicates, and asking which of the resulting predicates is true of a. Here, then, are instructions for forming the concept of an object. We will use a as our example.

Forming the Concept of an Object by "Contraction"

1. Choose a **subject** (or "creature") to form (in this case a)

2. Find which **predicates** are true of the chosen subject (a)

3. Find the **relations** the subject (a) has to each object in **u**. This is done by putting each name in **L** into the second place of each relation, and asking which of the resulting predicates are true of the subject (a).
4. Put the *name of* the subject (the mark 'a') into the blank of the new predicates, and ask which of the resulting statements are **true statements**.

5. **List** all the true statements with a as subject which can be stated in **L**.

Thus we form the concept of a (in L). Remember that the concept of a (in a particular language L) is simply the list of all true sentences about a which can be stated (in L). Also, remember that the language L is simply a list of names, predicates, and relations (given above).

The maneuver in step 3 is what Cusa metaphorically refers to by the term 'contraction.'[35] The point is that in forming the concept of, say, $\underline{a}$, we cannot simply *ignore* the other objects. Forming the concept of $\underline{a}$ *requires* reference to the other objects in $\underline{u}$ and to their relations to $\underline{a}$. Thus Cusa writes "...each creature receives all, so that in any creature all creatures are found in a relative way." Alternatively, we can think of the contraction of $\underline{a}$ as taking all possible statements in L and "huddling together" only the true statements about $\underline{a}$, and thus contracting the concept of $\underline{a}$, pulling it out, as it were, from the mass of possible statements in L.

So, $\underline{u}$, L, and our instruction for contraction are given above. Let's perform the contraction.

Forming the Concept of $\underline{a}$ by the Contraction of $\underline{u}$

1.   Subject: $\underline{a}$

2.   Predicates true of $\underline{a}$: $P_1(\underline{a}) = \underline{a}$ is a square.
                                                        $P_4(\underline{a}) = \underline{a}$ is a rectangle.

3.   Form relational predicates from relations R_1-R_3 by putting each name into the second place of each relation. The relations are

                $R_1 =$ ___ is to the left of ___ ,
                $R_2 =$ ___ is to the right of ___,
                $R_3 =$ ___ has more sides than ___.

And, after inserting each name into the second place of each relation we get the following predicates:

                $P_5 =$ ___ is to the left of $\underline{a}$,
                $P_6 =$ ___ is to the right of $\underline{a}$,
                $P_7 =$ ___ has more sides than $\underline{a}$.

                $P_8 =$ ___ is to the left of $\underline{b}$.
                $P_9 =$ ___ is to the right of $\underline{b}$.
                $P_{10} =$ ___ has more sides than $\underline{b}$.

                $P_{11} =$ ___ is to the left of $\underline{c}$.
                $P_{12} =$ ___ is to the right of $\underline{c}$.
                $P_{13} =$ ___ has more sides than $\underline{c}$.

                $P_{14} =$ ___ is to the left of $\underline{d}$.
                $P_{15} =$ ___ is to the right of $\underline{d}$.
                $P_{16} =$ ___ has more sides than $\underline{d}$.

                $P_{17} =$ ___ is to the left of $\underline{u}$.
                $P_{18} =$ ___ is to the right of $\underline{u}$.
                $P_{19} =$ ___ has more sides than $\underline{u}$.

---

[35]Perhaps it is better to say that *we* are metaphorically referring to contraction with the maneuver in step 3.

Exercises:

5. Write 'a' in the blanks of P5 - P19

6. Determine which of P1 - P19 are true of a, and below write out all true statements about a which are formulable in **L**. There are six.[36]

> a(i) $\underline{P_1(a)}$ = a is a square.
> a(ii) $\underline{P_4(a)}$ = a is a rectangle.
> a(iii) _____
> a(iv) _____
> a(v) _____
> a(vi) _____

We have formed (the concept of) a (in the language L) by contraction of **u**. The (concepts of the) other objects in **u** (b, c, d, and **u**) can be formed in the same way.

All in All and Each in Each

Now that we have formed a by contraction, we can ask in what sense all are in a and a is in each. Once we find this out, we can consider that the same is the case for all other objects in **u**. Thus we will see how this example illustrates Nicholas of Cusa's insight that "all is in all and each in each." First we have to define what it means in our example for one object to be "in" another.

DEFINITION II: *x is in y* = From the concept of *y* we can **deduce** the concept of *x*.[37]

This definition implies a number of important truths about the "in" relation. Among them are

> (i) Each thing is in itself.[38]
> (ii) If *x* is in *y*, and *y* is in *z*, then *x* is in *z*.

(Before going on, see that it is clear to you that (i) and (ii) follow from **DEF.II**.) Unfortunately, in constructing this example we had to make a sacrifice: simplicity or completeness. As you will see below, we will need a richer language in order to complete the demonstration that all are in all and each in each. We chose to save simplicity, and hint at how a complete example would have gone had the language L been complex enough.

What we need to show is that all is in all and each is in each. Showing how all is in a, and a is in each would be a first step, and then we could generalize from that case. From **DEF.I** and **DEF.II** we can define what it would be to show that all is in a and a is in all.

---

[36]Very interestingly, a circle can be seen as having either infinitely many sides or zero sides. (We are using 'sides' to mean 'edges.') We are supposing that the circle has infinitely many sides.

[37]We see from this definition that 'in' is not meant here in a spatial sense, but in a logical sense. We need to keep this in mind to see the relevance of this example to Cusa's view of the universe, for he is not saying that everything is (spatially) inside everything else.

[38]From this we see that **u** is also in itself. So, when we refer to "all objects in **u**" this includes **u** as well as a, b, c, and d

DEFINITION III: To show that all is in x and x is in all =

>(1) Derive all that can be said about **u**, **a**, **b**, **c**, and **d** (in **L**) from the concept of x (in **L**) (this would show that all are in x), and
>(2) Derive the concept of x from the concept of **a**, and from the concept of **b**, and from the concept of **c**, and from the concept of **d**, and from the concept of **u** (this would show that x is in all).

Let's consider proving that **b**, the triangle in **u**, is in **a**, the square. (Obviously the triangle is not spatially inside the square. Recall our point in footnote #18). The concept of **b** (in **L**) includes

> b(i) <u>b is a triangle.</u>
> b(ii) <u>b is to the right of a.</u>

Thus, to show that **b** is in **a** we need to derive b(i) and b(ii) (as well as all other true statements about **b** formulable in **L**) from a(i)-a(vi), the concept of **a**.. b(ii) is derivable from '**a** is to the left of **b**' (which is one of a(i)-a(vi)). Recall what you learned in Chapter 7 about the structure of arguments. In this case we can form an argument with "**a** is to the left of **b**" as the only premise, and b(i) as conclusion.

> (1) a is to the left of b.
> ----------------------------
> (2) <u>b</u> is to the right of <u>a</u>.

(2) follows from (1). For, if **a** is to the left of **b**, then **b** must be to the right of **a**.

b(i), however, is not derivable from the concept of **a** (i.e. a(i)-a(vi)) given the limited assortment of predicates and relations in **L**. We need a richer language to perform such a derivation. So, if we *extend* the language **L** and create a richer language **L'** by adding new predicates or relations to **L**, more and more of the concept of **b** will be derivable from the concept of **a**. (Also, the concepts of all objects in **u** will become richer, i.e. there will be more to say about them in **L'** than there is to say about them in **L**, and thus more statements in the lists which constitute their concepts).

Creating A Richer Language

Let's add the predicates P_{20} and P_{21} to **L** so we can perform the deduction of b(i) from a(i)-a(vi).

> **L': L** + P_{20} + P_{21}

> P_{20} = ___ is the only shape left of the triangle.
> P_{21} = ___ is the only shape left of **b**.

We can now add

> a(vii) <u>a is the only shape left of the triangle.</u>
> a(viii) <u>a is the only shape left of b.</u>

to the concept of **a**, and infer that **b** is a triangle, and so deduce b(i) from the (new and improved) concept of **a**. For, if we know that **a** is the only shape left of **b**, and **a** is also the only shape left of the triangle, then we know that **b** is the very next shape to the right of **a** and that the very next shape to the right of **a** is a triangle. Thus we know that **b** is that shape, a triangle.

So, by creating a richer language, the concepts of things are enriched and the relations between them are clearer in that more facts about all other objects are derivable from knowledge of any one of them. Above we extended **L** to **L'** by adding two predicates to **L**.

Using the (enriched) concept of a, we then derived a truth about b which we could not derive before in **L**, namely b(i). Were we to add more and more (of the right) predicates and/or relations, the concepts would become richer and richer, and more and more about b would be derivable from the concept of a. We leave it to you to imagine **L'** being extended to yet a richer language **L''** such that *all* truths about b (in **L''**) can be derived from the concept of a (in **L''**). Below we characterize Cusa's mystical philosophy as tantamount to the claim that in an *infinitely* rich language there is a single infinite concept which is at once the concept of *everything* (the whole) *and* the concept of *each thing* (each part taken separately) In essence, such a concept makes every individual an "exploded view" of the entire universe and everything in it.

An Exploded View† of the Universe

Now that we have defined the concept of contraction in a precise way with our miniature universe, we can consider the relevance of the above discussion to Cusa's view of the (real) universe. Again, in the terms of this example we can express Cusa's claims that in the infinite "everything is everything" and "all is in all and each in each" as follows: in an *infinitely rich* language, i.e. a language with infinitely many (of the right) predicates and relations, there is an infinite concept, i.e. an infinitely long list of true statements, which is at once the concept of *everything* (the whole) *and* the concept of *each thing* (each part taken separately). So, each predicate that is true of the universe considered as a whole, will be true of each individual object within the universe. Thus every predicate that is true of the universe as whole, will be true of the Leaning Tower of Pisa, the planet Venus, your left eyeball, and so on for every single object in the universe. (Recall Cusa's geometrical metaphor; if a circle is blown up to be infinitely large, Cusa says, it will become an infinite line and an infinite triangle and an infinite ellipse, etc.)

Of course, this probably sounds very strange. But, then again, it should! We do not possess an infinitely rich language. And could we ever have one? And could we understand what could be said in such a language? Only by a type of mystical insight that Cusa calls "learned ignorance."

Learned Ignorance

Nicholas of Cusa claimed that in the infinite all opposites become *unities* (not just that they become *consistent* or *compatible*). We don't see them as such, he says, because the items of our understanding are finitudes, and reason is discursive (that is, proceeds step by step). Rational criticism is a discursive process; it proceeds step by step. So, on this view, it can never lead to the ultimate truth. We cannot, by rational criticism, construct the *infinitely* rich language in which all opposites are *unified* and everything is seen to be everything. Rational criticism cannot give birth to the infinite concept which is at once the concept of everything (the whole) and of each thing (each part taken separately). Rational criticism is a process of finite steps, and you can take as many finite steps as you'd like. But, after any finite number of steps, you'll never be one step away from infinity. (There is no finite number n, such that n plus one equals infinity.) In fact, not only will no finite step take you from the finite into the infinite, *you'll never even get any closer at all! You'll never be just one step away. You'll always have infinitely many more steps to go!*

What, then, are we to do? Give up rational criticism? No. Recall how Kolak explains Cusa's concept of "learned ignorance": "...only through struggling in our efforts to understand the world do we realize precisely how and why the absolute truth about God, the world, and even our own natures, transcends our understanding". Thus, in order to fully realize the truth that everything is everything, and to understand things as such, we cannot give up rational criticism. Exactly the opposite: we have to push it beyond its limits. We have to overload the circuitry, not unplug the machine.

---

†Exploded view: An illustration or diagram of a construction, showing its parts separately, but in positions indicating their proper relations to the whole. (From the American Heritage Dictionary of the English Language.)

Chapter 9

The Copernican Revolution

Philosophical Evolution vs. Dogmatic Substitution

Was the transition from the geocentric theory of planetary motion, to the heliocentric theory, an example of philosophical evolution? The thrust of Chapter 9 of *Lovers of Wisdom* is that this transition should be viewed not as a philosophical evolution, but rather as a dogmatic substitution. Philosophical evolution implies a deepening of understanding. But when we replaced the geocentric theory with the heliocentric one there was not such philosophical advancement in the general case. Rather, the transition from the geocentric to the heliocentric view was, for most, simply a switch -- a replacement -- of one dogma with another. A scientific dogma replaced a religious one.

At most, empirical investigation reveals that the earth and sun move in relation to one another. Yet, for unclear reasons, it is believed by many that the scientific enterprise (with its high-powered empirical observation) has revealed that the heliocentric theory is *the* correct view. What many fail to realize, however, is that there is no fact of the matter as to whether the heliocentric or the geocentric theory is *the* correct one. Perhaps quite shockingly, asking which one of these theories is true, is as absurd as asking what the duck/rabbit picture (see Chapter 5 above) is *really* a picture of -- a duck or a rabbit. It is not simply that we are unsure which theory is correct (heliocentric vs. geocentric), it is that there is no feature of the world that makes one true *over the other*. Both the heliocentric and the geocentric models of the solar system consistently and equally well explain the observable planetary phenomena. So on what basis can we say that exactly one of these theories is true? One might be inclined to say that the correct theory is the "better" one. But what do we mean by "better?" If by "better" we mean simpler, then there doesn't seem to be a clear answer, as you learned in *Lovers of Wisdom*. If by "better" we mean works better for some specific purpose, then the answer seems to be context dependent. But even if we are precise about in what sense a theory can be better than another, "better" does not necessarily constitute truth. So the question still remains -- which theory is right? There is no fact of the matter.

There is, though, a philosophical lesson to be learned from the Copernican revolution. The revolution created the opportunity to be philosophically enlightened. It is our hope that you will seize this opportunity in the present section.

Let us here guide you to literally see the heliocentric reality. This does not mean that we will *prove* that the heliocentric view of the solar system is uniquely correct. For, one can also see the geocentric reality. In other words, we can perceive precisely the same planetary motions in one case as a heliocentric solar system and in another case as a geocentric solar system. (Recall the distinction between "seeing" and "seeing as" from Chapter 5 above.) The point is that it seems most of us have accepted the heliocentric view on faith. Let's do at least as well as those who thought that they could see that the geocentric theory was true. Let's look into the night sky and see ourselves move around the sun. If this can be done, then at least two things will be achieved. First, it will be *perceived* by you (perhaps for the first time) that the heliocentric explanation really is an explanation of the planetary motions. Second (and consequently), since Kolak enabled you (perhaps for the first time) to perceive the night sky in the geocentric way, you will be in a position to be philosophically enlightened. That is, you will not only believe Kolak's claim that neither view serves to characterize reality uniquely, but you will see for yourself that observation can underdetermine the correct theory of what is being observed. Even if you are not quite sure where this leaves us, you will be all the wiser. You will be making explicit to yourself an implicit feature of the reality in which you live.

Step 1

Get online. Go to the website at

http://www.perkins-observatory.org/2000.columns/1-16-2000

There you will find information about which planets are visible in the night sky between June and December of 2000. For information regarding what is visible in 2001, go to

http://www.perkins-observatory.org/column.html

There you should find a link with the updated information.

Step 2

Go out into the night, and chart what you see in the sky. You will need a pen and some paper, and you will need to be in a wide open area that allows you to see most of the sky after sundown. Now, find the biggest, brightest stars. Next, draw an outline of the horizon and position the brightest stars in relation to the horizon and one another. Then, plot the stars just dimmer than those. No need to represent all the stars you see. Devise a simple convention for representing degrees of illumination. For example, you might draw asterisks of different sizes. Here is an example of one such representation of the night sky:

Figure 1

Figure 1 is probably not what *you* will see. The brightest stars in the sky change their positions drastically, even over the course of one month.

Step 2

Get online again. Go to the website at

http://www.fourmilab.ch/cgi-bin/uncgi/Solar

Further instructions are provided there for retrieving a heliocentric interpretation of the solar system for the night of your observation. Here is an example of one such interpretation:

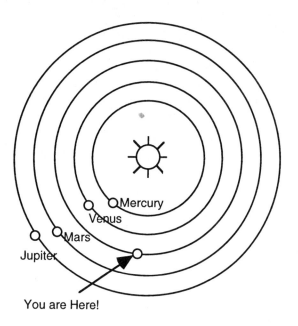

Figure 2

Print out a copy of the heliocentric interpretation for the date of *your* visual recording.

Step 3

On a new sheet of paper, construct a modified version of your recorded night-sky observation. This diagram should be drawn from the same perspective from which your night-sky observation was drawn. However, this diagram should also include the informativeness of the heliocentric diagram. The visible planets should be labeled, and their orbits around the sun should be plotted. Here, for example, would be such a diagram based on the above figures 1 and 2:

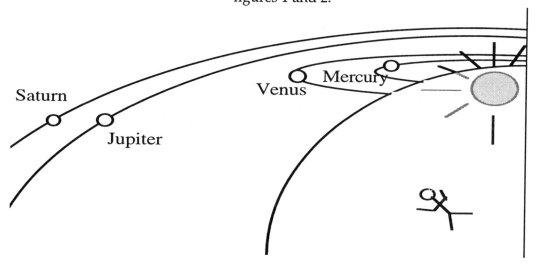

Figure 3

The new diagram represents what one should now see when she looks into the night sky. One should see various planets, and their heliocentric relation to one another. One should see our own position in the heliocentric solar system. That is, one should see our path around the sun, and see the relation of the earth's orbit to the orbits of the other planets. Yes, we should literally *see* the planets and the earth orbit around the sun, in the same sense that people used to see the sun revolve around the earth.

Step 4
After you have completed step 3, go back outside to the same spot and attempt to see your heliocentric position in the galaxy by simply looking at the stars.

Perception and Underdetermination
The possibility of this newly found perception should not be surprising. Consider the following scenario. You are in the driver's seat of what seems to be a parked car, and there is a tractor trailer next you, apparently parked. You have both halted for a red traffic-light. Suddenly, you perceive motion. Your car and the truck are perceived by you to be moving very slowly relative to one another. But are you rolling backward, or is the truck rolling forward? You slam on the brakes, thinking that you must have released your foot ever so slightly from them. But much to your surprise, the brakes are already locked. The truck is then perceived by you to be moving forward.

In this case, one's visual perception *underdetermines* the answer to the question of who is moving. In other words, the visual perception alone does not convey enough information to determine which is moving, your car or the truck. It is only after background information is presented that the eyes show you one thing rather than another. Initially, when you perceive yourself as moving, the background information includes the fear of hitting the car behind you. Then, the background information changes: you finally realize that your brakes are locked. At this point, you begin to perceive the truck moving. Such background theories inform the perceiver about what she is perceiving. Ultimately, that is how vision works. Ultimately that is how all perception works. In other words, background theories influence what you perceive things *as*. Perception is a complicated process of observation and theory.

In the imagined scenario, we say that there is a fact of the matter as to who is really moving, since the truck is moving *relative to the road*, and your car is not. The road is a relevant point of reference in this context. It cannot ultimately be ignored when trying answer the question of who is really moving. In the planetary case, however, it is not clear that there are any factors that everyone takes to be relevant regardless of the context. In other words, what feature of the solar system is analogous to the road (and its indispensability in deciding whether the car or truck is moving)? There is no such feature! It is only after the provision of further information, beliefs, concepts, experience etc. that one interpretation is preferred over another.

At one time people believed that the geocentric theory was true. They noticed that the earth and the sun moved relative to one another. They believed that if the earth moved, they would feel it.[39] They felt no such movement, and hence, concluded that the sun moved and that they *saw* it move. We are claiming, with Kolak, that they did in fact see this. They saw that the geocentric view was *a* correct explanation of planetary revolutions. Similarly, the above four step procedure enables us to see that the heliocentric view is also a correct explanation of the planetary motions. (We do mean 'see,' as in visually perceive.) But, observation underdetermines which of the two models is the "correct" one. Seeing the world does not amount to simply opening one's eyes, while passively taking in objective reality. Nor does it amount to simply opening one's eyes while passively experiencing a subjective reality. It is much more complicated mix of detection and projection. Perception depends not just on what is given based on your eyes, but on what you expect to see, what you are interested in finding out, which background theory are informing you, etc.

But, how exactly, and more precisely does perception work? And so, how is it that we come to know things? If we can acquire knowledge of the world around us, how should we do

---

[39]Imagine how shocked they would be to find out not only that the earth *moves*, but that relative to the sun it moves at an incredible average speed of 66,600 miles per hour (or 97,680 feet per second)!

56

it, especially given what we now know about the underdetermination of theory (now that we are philosophically enlightened)? What methods of justification are legitimate, if we want to track the truth? Maybe as some of the ancient skeptics thought, we really can't know anything. Can we know anything? Maybe knowledge is only apparent, and we are forever severed from objective reality as it is in itself! These are some of the questions that we should be asking ourselves. They are some of the key questions asked by the philosophers discussed in the next seven chapters. Their movement is called modern philosophy, of which Descartes is said to be the father.

Descartes knew his history. He read the works of Galileo, the Medieval philosophers and the ancient Greeks. In fact, Descartes was of the first generation of western philosophers, after the fall of the Roman Empire, to have translations of virtually all the ancient Greek texts that we have translated today. With such an arsenal of philosophical history, and with the opportunity for philosophical enlightenment provided by the Copernican revolution, Descartes began his philosophical journey.

Chapter 10

Descartes

A Philosophical Experiment

Are you comfortable? Are you distracted? Then go to a quiet place. Satisfy your desires, if you have any, then come back. If you are hungry, go eat. If you are cold, put on warmer clothing. If the lighting is causing you to wince, adjust it. You are about to embark upon a philosophical journey once embarked upon by Descartes. He began by freeing himself of all cares. Therefore, so must you. Furthermore, you must be alone. You must be isolated. This is not a communal activity. This is all you. In fact, you don't even need your body for this one. Ignore it. Again, this is much easier without the distractions of everyday life. So, find the time to put them aside and forget about them during the exercise. If you cannot do this, put the book down and try again later. Most importantly, do not try to hurry through this section. Just be here. If you really do exist, then this should not be very difficult and the conclusions to be drawn will not be too alarming. Are you ready? Are you sure? Then begin.

Your exercise is to find an unshakable foundation for all knowledge. Knowledge is traditionally conceived as a justified, true belief. So if we *know* x, then we believe x, we have good reason to believe x, and x is true. Accordingly, Descartes argued that our knowledge is only as strong as its foundation (as its ultimate justification). When the foundation is weak, so is everything that rests upon it. You may think that you know that it is safe to walk through Central Park at 2:00 am. But if your belief rests on, say, wishful thinking, then your alleged knowledge is tenuous. On the other hand, if your belief rests upon the impeccable word of some experienced and truthful authority, then your alleged knowledge is beginning to look much more secure. Descartes set out to secure human knowledge, but he strived for a higher level of security. He strived for absolute certainty. Your present activity, then, is the same as one once undertaken by Descartes -- that of locating an unshakable foundation for all human knowledge. Find a truth that cannot be doubted, and you will have succeeded.

Start out easy. Answer the following question. Does Joe Salerno exist? His name is on the cover of this book. Do you know that he exists? Maybe. We know that you think you know that Joe Salerno exists. But are you certain? Might it not be false that he exists? Certainly. For all you know, the name was made up and he did not help us write this supplement to *Lovers of Wisdom*. What makes you think he exists? The cover of the book says so. Do you always believe what you read? Do books ever contain false propositions? Often. If it is possible that your belief about Joe is false, then it is not absolutely certain. But then such a belief cannot serve as the kind of foundation that Descartes was looking for. So it is not the kind of foundation that we are in search of. Throw it out. Do not believe that Joe Salerno exists. In fact, treat it as highly suspect. That is Descartes' method, the method of doubt. *De omnibus dubitandum est*: doubt everything that can be doubted!

Did Descartes check each and every belief to determine whether it could be doubted before he abandoned it? No. He rid himself of doubtable beliefs *en masse*, as you are about to do. Has an authority ever deceived you? Who have been the authorities in your life? Parents? Teachers? Religious figures? Police officers? Authors? What are their track records like? Have they ever been mistaken, or expressed a falsehood, or lied? Have they ever deceived you, purposefully or unintentionally? Have their assertions been unreliable in any way? In other words, are they fallible? If so, disregard everything they have ever told you. Authority is not a guide to absolute certainty, since an authority can be wrong. Acquiring belief through authority is, at best, slightly better than hearsay. Hearsay is not a guide to absolute irrefutability. Take Descartes' advice and throw out everything we have come to believe that has as its source an authority figure.

What about your senses? Have they ever deceived you? Try to remember. Have you ever seen a mirage? Did you ever mistake someone for someone else? What about pink elephants with purple polka dots? Have you seen any of them in your overly festive moments? Many have. But many have misperceived. Unless your senses have an unprecedented 100% reliability record, discard all your perceptual beliefs. We suggest that you remain seated for this one. Suppose that the table in front of you does not exist. Those are not your hands, and there is no color in the world. If you drop this book it will not fall to the ground, and in fact, no such book exists. Nor do any of the objects around you exist. Suppose that the entire world that you are perceptually aware of is, at best, one giant hallucination.

Descartes began there. He argued from past illusions to the uncertainty of present perceptions. Are you convinced? It's hard to deny that there is a book in front of you. Here it is! Ah, but Descartes also thought of that. Have you not found yourself in situations which seemed as real as this one, only to later find that you had been dreaming? We bet you have. For all you know, you, right now, are dreaming. Go ahead, pinch yourself. Ask yourself whether this is all just a dream. Well? If you did not really pinch yourself, please, put the book down and try it. Did it hurt? We bet it did! What do you think that shows? Did you ask yourself whether this experience, that you are now having, is a dream? If not, please, stop reading for a moment and ask. Well? We bet that you think you are really awake. You know what? You are probably right. But what if you were dreaming? What would the pinch have felt like? Would it have hurt? It might! Would you not think this was all real, even if it were a dream? You might! Admit it. The point is that there is no way to verify it *absolutely*. It is doubtable that all this, here, in front of you is real -- that is, it can all be doubted. It is possible that you are wrong about the "reality" around you. Every single belief that you have acquired through your senses is doubtable. That is what Descartes' argument from dreams is supposed to show, that your perceptual beliefs are not indubitable. And this is so, because there no possible test that can prove conclusively that your are not now dreaming. And so, none of your perceptual beliefs can serve as the foundation for all of your knowledge. None can act as the support on which all other knowledge rests.

So far you have not found any indubitable beliefs. If there are none, then it is not clear that we have any knowledge at all. Descartes wrote,

> I will continue ... in this track until I shall find something that is certain, or at least, if I can do nothing more, until I shall know with certainty that there is nothing certain.[40]

And so shall we continue.

Wait a minute! Before we go anywhere, are you going to let us get away with this much? We just asked you to drop *everything* that you believe about the spatial-temporal world! You no longer have hands. There are no colors. You did not come from where you think you came from. It is not the year you think it is. There are no years. Rocks, trees and tables are figments of your imagination. Nobody wrote these words, and there is no Earth. There are no other people, no objects at all. There is no physical space. Are you trying to disregard these beliefs? Are you a lunatic? Are we mad for hypothesizing such falsity? Is Descartes out of his mind? He actually did this in his pajamas! Isn't he supposed to be this really smart guy? He corresponded with scholars and Queens, attended the finest universities and traveled afar. He discovered analytic geometry and developed a physics that competed with Sir Isaac Newton's. What is going on?

Ah, the key question: "what was Descartes doing?" Why are we demolishing so much of our belief system in the way that Descartes did? Surely, if Descartes wanted to deny everything once and for all, he could not survive. Could we? Luckily, you're sitting down. Otherwise, if you were successful in ridding yourself of your perceptual beliefs, you might hurt

---

[40]First paragraph of *Meditation II*.

59

yourself. Surely you could not survive for very long. Surely, you would be out of your mind! Descartes did not fail to see this. He wrote,

> ...how could I deny that I possess these hands and this body, and withal escape being classed with persons in a state of insanity, whose brains are so disordered and clouded by dark bilious vapours as to cause them pertinaciously to assert that they are monarchs when they are in the greatest poverty; or clothed [in gold] and purple when destitute of any covering; or that their head is made of clay, their body of glass, or that they are gourds? I should certainly be not less insane then they, were I to regulate my procedure according to examples so extravagant.[41]

What, then, was Descartes doing? What are you doing? Do you know the answer? Maybe we should read the *Meditations* again. Remember, Descartes is not a skeptic. He is not raising the skeptical challenge that "what can be false probably is, and you cannot prove otherwise." Furthermore, he is not arguing that we should live our lives in such doubt. Rather he is saying that whatever can be doubted is not absolutely certain, and therefore cannot serve as an unshakable foundation for the superstructure of knowledge. The point of shoveling all these dubious beliefs out the window is to see what remains (if anything) when the shoveling is complete. If we end up with something when the shoveling is done, maybe we can build upon it. Descartes was optimistic on this score, and so his skepticism was *instrumental* to building an indubitable foundation for knowledge. But please, continue *your* search.

Maybe mathematics can be the foundation. It should be no surprise that Descartes entertained this possibility. He was a mathematician. Consider your belief that $2+3=5$, or your belief that a square has four sides. Are these beliefs doubtable? Are you certain that $2+3=5$? Prove it! Here are two things: **. And here are three things: ***. Count them up. What did you get? Five? Maybe you made a mistake in your counting? Is that even remotely possible? Could you have been mistaken each time that you tried in the past to add two and three? Is there the slightest chance of this? Maybe everyone who has ever checked your math was also mistaken by overlooking your mistakes. Clearly there is no contradiction involved in the hypothesis that you have just now, and have always, been mistaken in your counting. If this is right, then arithmetic beliefs are not absolutely undoubtable by you. Similar problems are had by your geometrical beliefs, and by your mathematical beliefs generally. Descartes asked,

> ...how do I know that I am not also deceived each time I add together two and three, or number the sides of a square, or form some judgment still more simple, if more simple indeed can be imagined?[42]

Answer: you do not know, not with absolute certainty anyway.

Let's try to get clear on the sense in which mathematical claims are doubtable. Notice that to deny a mathematical claim is absurd, that is, it is to commit oneself to a contradiction.

> Suppose $2+3\neq5$. Now $2=1+1$, and $3=1+1+1$. So $2+3=1+1+1+1+1$. But $1+1+1+1+1=5$. So $2+3=5$. But we just said $2+3\neq5$. Therefore, both $2+3=5$ and $2+3\neq5$. Contradiction!

If to deny a mathematical claim is to end in contradiction, then surely it is not rational to deny it. We may confidently conclude, then, that in fact $2+3=5$. Yet, for Descartes, such confidence does not a solid foundation make. After all, we might have made a mistake in our proof that

---

[41]See *Meditation I.*
[42]See *Meditation I.*

2+3≠5 implies a contradiction. The sense of understanding and certainty you have toward the mathematical claim may be, for all you know, a false sense. In the same way that a mathematician might be able to dupe us by walking us through a very complicated, long proof, an evil demon could easily dupe us as we stroll through a very simple, short proof, like the one presented above. Such a demon could make us think that we understand even when there is no real understanding going on. The sense of understanding is, after all, just a feeling. Can we not have the feeling while being totally misguided? Many people do. If any steps are to be taken or if there is any distance whatsoever between you and the truth of the belief, then it could, for all you know, be false -- and so, is not certain knowledge.

Descartes must have been in search of the strongest sense of understanding and certainty possible. He was in search of a kind of grasp that was enough in and of itself to guarantee the truth in question. What would such grasp be like? What kind of truth has this characteristic of making it impossible to be denied? An example of a sentence with this property may be helpful. Consider the following sentence (call it S1).

(S1)   "S1 is a false sentence."

You cannot really deny (S1). To do so is to say, "it is false that 'S1 is a false sentence.'" In other words, it is to say that S1 is true. The point is that in denying S1 you are committed to the truth of S1. To deny it is to undermine your denial. S1 has this strange property. Descartes has something like this sort of property in mind when he seeks an "irrefutable" sentence, a sentence that cannot be doubted without canceling that very doubt.

But, if you think that you can stop here, and take S1 as the foundational truth, think again. Though it has this very virtuous property of being impossible to deny, there is a down side -- it also has the property of being impossible to *affirm*! To affirm its truth is to undermine that very affirmation. Suppose that S1 is true. Then what it says obtains, namely, that S1 is false. But then its truth secures its falsity.

S1 is an anomaly. It is not clear what we should make of it. Given the task at hand, we should shelve S1 for the time being. Hopefully, though, the attention we paid to it has focused our search. We are in search of a belief, the denial of which secures its truth, but whose truth does not entail its falsity. Notice that we could not be wrong about such a truth. We cannot make a mistake in coming to know it, and to entertain the possibility that it is false only guarantees its truth.

Before you go on, let us summarize. You have encountered the *argument from illusions* and the *argument from dreams,* both of which were intended by Descartes to show that all of our perceptual beliefs might be false. Then we encountered the *evil demon argument*. Descartes hoped to show with this argument that all our mathematical beliefs might be false. The evil demon was hypothesized by Descartes in order to make the point that a feeling of understanding and certainty is not enough to guarantee knowledge, even in the simplest mathematical cases. A simple sense of certainty does not absolute certainty make. What makes for absolute certainty is a sentence, the entertaining of which by you makes it irrefutable by you. For in thinking the sentence, you preclude its falsity.

What about your own existence? Can you be wrong about that? Close your eyes and say to yourself, "I do not exist." Please, try to sincerely assert this proposition to yourself. Does the denial of your own existence undermine itself? Surely you can coherently deny the existence of, say, Joe Salerno, since, for all you know, he really does not exist. But when you think the words "I do not exist" the "I" refers to the person doing the thinking. Such a thinker exists, otherwise the words would not have been thought. Therefore, when you think "I do not exist," you falsify that sentence. So you cannot deny your own existence without undermining that denial. Similarly, as long as you *think* you exist, you do. For someone must be doing the thinking

Hogwash! This is just a bunch of philosophical theorizing. The above explanation is anything but simple. Surely, the reasoning behind the certainty of "I exist" is much more complicated than the reasoning behind the certainty of "2+3=5". If the evil demon could deceive us about the later, surely he could deceived us about the former. Right? Couldn't he deceive you about your own existence? Is there any distance between your utterance "I exist" and the fact of your own existence itself. Remember, in the mathematical case, there were steps in a proof that were needed to ultimately justify simple mathematical claims. Such intermediary steps established the possibility (even if remote) of making a mistake, or of being duped. There was distance between a mathematical utterance and its ultimate justification or truth maker. Suppose that the evil demon was right now deceiving you about everything he could possibly deceive you about. Would this include the deception about your own existence? Are there any steps or intermediaries between your own thinking and you the thinker. Descartes thought not. He writes,

> Doubtless, then, I exist, since I am deceived; and let him deceive me as he may, he can never bring it about that I am nothing, so long as I shall be conscious that I am something. So that it must ... be maintained ... that this proposition: I am, I exist, is necessarily true each time it is expressed by me, or conceived in my mind.[43]

Exercises:

1.   Is Descartes right about this? He says that he indubitably exists, since he is deceived. What is Descartes' point here? Determine whether you could be wrong about your own existence. Could the evil demon really never deceive you about your own existence? Why or why not?

2.   Note that even if it is impossible to consistently deny one's own existence, not much (if anything at all) immediately follows about *what* one is. For instance, if above you concluded that you must exist, perhaps you gave a sigh of relief as to say "*I exist! I am* real! I really *am* here, not dreaming. I *have* hands! I *have* a book before me! It's all *true!*" If so, you let in too much too soon. The impossibility of denying your own existence does not prove that you are not dreaming, or that you have hands, or that you are male or female, or that you are a human being, or that a physical world exists, or that 2+3=5, or that...(perhaps every other thing we ordinarily take as plainly and unquestionably true). Once Descartes convinced himself that he existed, he probably rolled right over and went to sleep, feeling he had done a good night's work. But, he did not stop there. On his subsequent days of meditation, he took a great deal of time *building* on the foundation of "I exist." Ask yourself what, if anything, really follows from the proposition "I [meaning *you*] exist." Explain.

---

[43]See *Meditation II.*

Chapter 11

Spinoza

How to Read Spinoza

Spinoza presents his insights in a format unlike any other philosopher discussed in *Lovers of Wisdom*. So, naturally, you'll have to acquire the insights from his work by a unique procedure. In this chapter we will not summarize Spinoza's views. Rather, we will outline a recipe for excavating Spinoza's insights from his geometric-style arguments. By following it you will be making Spinoza's philosophy explicit to yourself.

We suggest that you read Spinoza's selection in the following way:

1. Read the "propositions," but skip the "demonstrations."

2. Read the "definitions" and "axioms" without pausing to clarify details. Just read through them swiftly.

3. Read the propositions again, this time more closely, and this time read the demonstrations as well. When the demonstrations refer to definitions, axioms, or earlier propositions, go back to the definitions, axioms and propositions to read them carefully.

4. After you read a given proposition and its accompanying demonstration etc., write a sentence or short paragraph putting that proposition into your own words. If you find that it helps you, be informal as you write these sentences. Try to write them in such a way that you can hear yourself *saying* them to someone. Make them feel as "natural" as you can. Use whatever idiosyncratic expressions you prefer. For now, forget about whether you have him "*right*" or not. Just try to capture what it seems to you that Spinoza is saying. Have fun with it.

Paraphrases of *Ethics*, Book I: "Of God"
PROPOSITION I:
PROPOSITION II:
PROPOSITION III:
PROPOSITION IV:
PROPOSITION V:
PROPOSITION VI:
PROPOSITION VII:
PROPOSITION VIII:
PROPOSITION XXV:
PROPOSITION XXXII:
PROPOSITION XXXIII:

Exercises:
1.   The notions of attribute and mode are related but should not be confused. Distinguish these two notions given in definitions IV and V in your own words.
   Attribute:
   Mode:

2.   Consider the following list of substances and characteristics. For each pair determine whether the given characteristic is an attribute or mode of the given substance. (It may be helpful to recall the discussion of Aristotle's view of substance as form plus matter, and the corresponding explanation of essential and accidental characteristics. See Chapter 3 above)

	Substance	Characteristic	Attribute/Mode
(a)	God	Existence	_____
(b)	Aristotle	Existence	_____
(c)	You	Human being	_____
(d)	You	Reader of *Lovers of Wisdom*	_____
(e)	Fire	Heat	_____
(f)†	God	You	_____

3.   How is the quotation from Plotinus (at the start of this chapter) related to Spinoza's world-view?

4.   Paraphrase Spinoza's selection from *Ethics* Book I ("Of God") in a standard prose form. Use your sentences from step 4 of the reading procedure above as a start. Take any metaphors or idiosyncratic expressions you used in those sentences and explain them as clearly as you can, explicitly relating them to Spinoza's terminology. Try to encompass as many of his propositions and their demonstrations as you can in your summary, but mainly attend to the following:

Proposition I. Substance is prior to its modifications.

Proposition III. If two things have nothing in common with one another, one
                    cannot be the cause of the other.

Proposition VI. One substance cannot be produced by another substance.

Proposition VII. It pertains to the nature of substance to exist.

Proposition VIII. Every substance is necessarily infinite.

You then will have made Spinoza explicit to yourself.

---

† (f) is more difficult than (a)-(e) since it may not be clear how you are *either* an attribute or mode of God, let alone *which* you are. Consideration of Spinoza's world-view is required.

Chapter 12

Leibniz

Leibnizian Principles

As Kolak mentions in Chapter 12 of *Lovers of Wisdom*, Leibniz wrote no single work that contains a definitive statement of his understanding of the world. Rather, his most important ideas are preserved in many short works and letters. It is possible, however, to give a general picture of the core of Leibniz's philosophy, the theory of monads, by discussing three principles central to this theory.[44] Each of these principles is discussed, either explicitly or implicitly, in the selection from the *Monadology* in Chapter 12 of *Lovers of Wisdom*. In this chapter we will clarify each of them.

The three principles are:

(i) The Principle of the Identity of Indiscernibles
(ii) The Predicate-in-Notion Principle[45]
(iii) The Mirroring Principle

The Principle of the Identity of Indiscernibles

The Principle of the Identity of Indiscernibles states that each individual, simple substance (whether actual or merely possible) can, in principle, be distinguished from all other individual substances. In short, this principle implies that there are no two things exactly alike: for any two monads it is possible to find some characteristic that distinguishes one from the other. Just as there are no two snowflakes that are exactly alike, according to Leibniz, no two monads are exactly alike. Thus, Leibniz's universe is full of an infinity of unique substances.

The 'Predicate-in-Notion' Principle

The 'predicate-in-notion' principle states that all predicates true of a given subject are part of the very concept (or "notion") of that subject. Think of your kitchen table. What can you predicate of this object? Perhaps it is brown, has four legs, is made of wood, is 4 years old, etc. According to Leibniz, the concept of your kitchen table consists in all of the predicates that are true of it. And, importantly, these predicates include everything that has ever happened to your table, everything that is now happening to your table, and everything that ever will happen to that table. But remember that Leibniz talks not of tables and chairs, but of *monads*. Thus, the concept of a monad consists in all of the predicates that are true of that monads. So, the concept of a monad includes everything that has ever happened to that monad, everything that is now happening to that monad, and everything that ever will happen to that monad.[46]

If you recall, in our discussion of "contraction" and the construction of the concept of an object (Chapter 8 above), we described the concept of an object (in a particular language)

---

[44]There are more principles that could be discussed in a detailed account of Leibniz's writings. Important examples are the Principle of Contradiction, and the Principle of Sufficient Reason. Each of these is mentioned explicitly in *Monadology* (§31 and §32 respectively). We will limit ourselves to discussing only three principles.

[45]This term was coined by C.D. Broad.

[46]The next step would be to state that whatever predicates *could be* true of a given subject are part of it's individual concept. This is a difficult issue to decide. For more on this question consider his distinction between absolute and hypothetical necessity discussed in the selection from *Monadology*.

as the list of all true statements that can be formed about the given object (in that language). We can use this idea once again to understand Leibniz. For Leibniz, the concept of some individual substance, such as, say, Leibniz himself, is a list -- an infinitely long list of predicates that are true of that individual substance. Importantly, the list of predicates that specifies the entire history of an individual substance is *eternally true* of that substance. For instance, the list of predicates that specify the history of your kitchen table *was* true of it even before it was created, and will be true of it even after it is destroyed. Similarly, the list of predicates that specify the history of Leibniz was true of him even before he was born, before his parents were born, before the earth even existed, and before anything you can think of. And, as above, this history of Leibniz will be true of Leibniz forever --even after he is dead. So, the concepts of individual substances are eternal and unchanging. In this sense they are like Platonic forms. The individual concept, then, is the eternal unchanging concept of the (changing) individual substance.[47]

More needs to be said about the list of predicates that comprise an individual concept. *Time* is crucial these predicates. In fact, these predicates, according to Leibniz, should include the most specific reference to time. Consider the statement "Leibniz was born in 1646." This statement is true. Therefore, according to the predicate-in-notion principle, the concept that individuates Leibniz from everything else includes the predicate "was born in 1646." Further, the fact that Leibniz *was* born in 1646 compels us to acknowledge that, from the point of view of events prior to 1646, the statement "Leibniz *will be* born in 1646" is true. So, the predicate "will be born in 1646" is part of the concept that individuates Leibniz from everything else. Finally, in 1646 while Leibniz was being born "Leibniz *is being* born (in 1646)" was true. So the predicate "is being born in 1646" is part of the concept that individuates Leibniz from everything else. The importance of this sort of time-indexing is to avoid contradictions. For instance, the predicates "is an infant" and "is not an infant" are contradictory. But the predicates "is an infant in 1646" and "is not an infant in 1700" are not contradictory. Both are true of Leibniz.

So, not only is each individual substance (or monad) unique (given the identity of indiscernibles), but their concepts also eternally contain their entire history (past, present and future). Thus, the concepts of individual substances are maximally packed with every bit of information about that substance, and every such concept is distinct from every other. From this we see that, though similar in many of their initial assumptions, Leibniz and Nicholas of Cusa reach diametrically opposed conclusions. Nicholas of Cusa (as we construed him in Chapter 8) believed that as our language approaches infinite enrichment, the concepts of things merge into a single infinite concept. Leibniz, on the other hand, thought that as our language approaches infinite enrichment the concepts of things divide, becoming more and more precise, until there are infinitely many distinct individual concepts. In Cusa's case, the concepts merge into a single "infinite sun," and in Leibniz's case, the concepts separate into an "infinity of suns."

The Mirroring Principle

The 'mirroring' principle states that each thing mirrors every other thing in the universe. This principle is very similar to Nicholas of Cusa's claim that "all is in all and each in each." An important difference between the two is that Leibniz makes clear that "mirroring" comes in *degrees*; each thing mirrors everything else, but mirrors some things more clearly than others. But what does it mean for mirroring to come in degrees? Consider how much a friend knows about you. Suppose that although she does know a great deal, she does not know everything about you. We say that she has *information* about you. But how precise is her information? Suppose that your parents know much more about you than your friend does. Then, relative to your friend, your parents have more precise information about you. So your parents "mirror" you more clearly than your friend. To be sure, Leibniz speaks of things that mirror

---

[47]Earlier, you may have read Chapter 2 on Plato's theory of forms. Did it cross your mind to ask if, in addition to forms of "tablehood" and "bookhood," there is a Platonic form of "_____ [your name]-hood?"

the *universe*. But our example illustrates the point that information comes in degrees. And it is this point that leads Leibniz to say that mirroring the universe comes in degrees of clarity.

Thus, a monad (M) mirrors the universe more clearly than another (N), if M contains more precise information about the universe than N does. Understanding the phenomenon of mirroring in this way, enables us to clearly see the parallel between Leibniz's mirroring principle, on the one hand, and Nicholas of Cusa's claim that "all is in all and each in each," on the other. Both men think that a single object (or monad) within the universe contains information about the entire universe (and hence everything within the universe), but only Leibniz thinks that information comes in degrees of clarity.

Exercises:
1. Summarize the Principle of the Identity of Indiscernibles, the Predicate in notion Principle, and the Mirroring Principle in your own words.
Identity of Indiscernibles:
Predicate-in-Notion:
Mirroring:

2.   Below is a description of an imaginary library. Think of the library as a metaphor for Leibniz's universe. Certain features of the library and its contents metaphorically correspond to the three Leibnizian principles discussed in this chapter.

> Imagine an infinite library. In it there are infinitely many books, with infinitely many words on each page of each book. Each book, marked with its own unique call number, is a book about the Infinite Library (the very library the books are in). The books are so detailed that a perfect librarian could pick up any one, open it to any page, and, from reading that page alone, could know what was on every page of every book in the library. A less skilled librarian reading a page of a book in the library, however, could only learn about the books near the one being read from. Further, there are no two pages exactly alike in the entire library. Therefore no two books are exactly alike. So, the Infinite Library is a library full of infinitely many books about itself, each telling a different story, yet including all the others.

There are parallels between the above description of an infinite library, and Leibniz's philosophy. For instance, one could say that the unique call number belonging to each book corresponds to the individual concept of a monad, and that each book corresponds to a monad. In the spaces below, identify the elements in the above description that correspond to the three principles discussed earlier. In other words, what aspects of the above description correspond to the Principle of the Identity of Indiscernibles, the Predicate-in-notion Principle, and the Mirroring Principle? Below is a key that will help you to see the basic parallels between this metaphor and Leibniz's metaphysics.[48]

Leibniz's Philosophy	*Infinite Library Metaphor*
The universe	Infinite Library
Monads	Books
States of monads -- i.e., "perceptions"	pages
Identity of Indiscernibles	_____
Predicate-in-notion	_____
Mirroring	_____

---

[48]Incidentally, Leibniz was a librarian. In 1690 he was appointed librarian at Wolfenbuttel, near Hanover. Perhaps he occupied himself with such thoughts while fulfilling his duties as librarian.

There are more parallels between Leibniz's views and the imaginary Infinite Library. See if you can find them. Also, try to add some more details to the story about the Infinite Library (or rewrite it altogether) to create analogs to other elements of Leibniz's philosophy.

Chapter 13

Locke

Locke and Descartes

John Locke's epistemology, we read, can be understood as a response to Descartes'. Both Descartes and Locke sought an ultimate foundation for knowledge. Both intended to build up from this their foundations to an aspiring theory of the world (Descartes intended to ground his own physics called "The World," whereas Locke intended to ground the physics of Isaac Newton). The two philosophers were in agreement in thinking that the structure of knowledge is only as strong as its foundation, and that something indubitable should serve as that foundation. They further agreed that such indubitability involved our own minds, since our minds are more directly known to us than anything else. Unlike Descartes, however, Locke took indubitability to inhere in the presentation of ideas themselves. In other words, Locke believed that it is undoubtable that we are having ideas. And it seem that he took the physical world to be the best explanation of where our ideas come from. Descartes, however, took the senses to be the most *un*reliable source of knowledge. Whereas Locke thought that the senses played a role in securing a foundation of certainty, Descartes denied this and argued that reason alone secures it.

An Epistemological Checklist

	Knowledge requires a foundation of certainty	Introspection is key to certainty	Certainty is rooted in ideas (given by the senses)	Certainty is rooted in thought (given by reason).
Descartes	√	√	X	√
Locke	√	√	√	X

In addition to providing different accounts of the nature of certainty, Kolak notes an further difference between the philosophies of Locke and Descartes. Locke's theory aims to have the further virtue of ontological economy. In other words, Locke's theory commits us to fewer metaphysically distinct kinds of things. So, Locke's theory, in the face of Descartes', satisfies the principle of Ockham's Razor. Remember, Ockham's Razor is the principle that, all else being equal, the simplest theory -- the one that requires commitment to the fewest numbers of entities -- should be accepted over its competitors. In this case, the competing theories are Locke's and Descartes' epistemologies -- their theories of knowledge. Both theories are intended to explain how knowledge is possible. Even if they explain equally well, Locke's has the virtue of ontologically economy. Locke acknowledges as much:[49]

Wielding Ockham's razor, Locke writes,

---

[49]For further detailed discussion of Ockham's Razor, its nature and the need for it, see the Appendix to Chapter 7 above.

> It is an established opinion ... that there are ... innate principles ...
> stamped upon the mind of man which the soul receives in its first
> being and brings into the world with it. It would be sufficient to
> convince unprejudiced readers of the falseness of this supposition,
> if I should only show (as I hope I shall...) how men...may attain to
> all the knowledge they have, without the help of any innate
> impressions, and may arrive at certainty, without any such original
> notions or principles.[50]

Eschewing the traditional acceptance of innate ideas (since it is ontologically indulgent), Locke takes his epistemology to have the virtue of ontological economy.

Recall that Descartes (in his second *Meditation*) required the existence of innate ideas to explain his knowledge that the wax at a time T2 is one and the same piece of wax perceived at some earlier time T1. Descartes was puzzled as to how he could know that the wax persisted over time, given that no aspect of the wax (of which he was consciously aware) remained unchanged from T1 to T2. How do we know that things that undergo change retain their identity? The question that Descartes raised about the wax extends to *anything* that undergoes change. And Descartes answers this question by positing the existence of innate ideas -- the very ideas that Locke disparages. Descartes also used innate ideas, if you recall, to explain how he knew that the beings walking in the square below his window were men and not automata. Thus, according to Locke, Descartes posited the existence of innate ideas to explain knowledge of both identity (unity over time) and kind (unity at a time). If Locke does in fact account for such types of knowledge without appealing to innate ideas and without adding any *new* mysterious entities, then his theory has the virtue being simpler than Descartes', while retaining the explanatory power of Descartes' theory. In such a case, according to the principle of Ockham's razor, Locke's theory is superior.

Is Locke's Epistemology Superior to Descartes'?

Is Locke's epistemology superior? Can we give up innate ideas and still account for (1) knowledge of *sameness* over time (e.g. that the piece of wax is the same piece over a change in time)? and (2) knowledge of what *kind* of thing something is (e.g. that something is a piece of wax versus a table or chair)? Locke was an empiricist. So he believed that all knowledge of the world was acquired through the senses.[51] He conceives of our knowledge as being constructed out of our ideas, all of which ultimately spring from our simple and most basic perceptions (such as, perceptions of redness, triangularity, heat, solidity, and motion). These simple ideas give birth to all other ideas through successive acts of reflection. On Locke's view, the compounding, comparing and abstracting of ideas, comprise these acts of reflection. So, given this empiricism, how does Locke account for (2); our knowledge of kind?

The problem of knowledge of kind is not a new one. Plato addressed it with his theory of forms; knowledge of kind, says Plato, is a recognition that some particular, sensible object "partakes in" some form (see Chapter 2 above). Plotinus addressed the question with his theory of *nous* ; knowledge of kind, says Plotinus, is made possible by the individuation of Platonic forms by the divine intellect (see Chapter 5 above). Aristotle addressed the question with his theory of the active and passive intellects; knowledge of kind, says Aristotle, is the abstraction of intelligible forms (by the active intellect) from encounters with particular objects (see Chapter 6 above). And, of course, Descartes addressed it with his theory of innate ideas.

Before plunging into a Lockean account of our knowledge of kind, stop to think about what Locke is supposed to be accounting for here. "Knowledge of kind" refers to the

---

[50]John Locke, *An Essay Concerning Human Understanding*, A. C. Fraser, ed. (Oxford: Clarendon Press, 1894), Bk. 1, chap. II, sec. 1.

[51]Locke did not think that *all* knowledge is acquired from the senses. According to him, we have a "threefold" knowledge of existence: we have knowledge of *our own* existence by intuition, we have knowledge of *God* by demonstration, and we have knowledge of (the physical) *world* by sensation. (See his *Essay Concerning Human Understanding*, Bk. IV, Ch. IX, Sec. 2.)

component of experience we have called (in Chapter 5) "perception *as*.." In recognizing what kind of thing some object is, you are not merely perceiving the object, but perceiving it *as* one sort of thing rather than another. You perceive the object as instantiating a certain property, say, "rabbithood." (Go back to the duck/rabbit discussion in Chapter 5 if you are having trouble remembering the distinction between "seeing" and "seeing as."). The question is, how does this "seeing as" occur?

Let us begin with a Lockean account of (1); knowledge of kind (seeing as). You will subsequently test it.

A Lockean Account of Knowledge of Kind

Locke was an empiricist. So he believed that all knowledge of the world is ultimately derived from the senses. Our knowledge of the world is constructed out of our ideas, all of which ultimately have as their source our simple and most basic perceptions (such as, perceptions of redness, triangularity, heat, solidity, and motion). From these simple ideas all other ideas are derived, by successive acts of *reflection*. Such acts exhaustively include, on Locke's view, the compounding, comparing and abstracting of ideas. The *simple ideas* are the most basic, unanalyzable perceptions given by the senses. The *complex ideas* are those based on the simple ones, but derived from them by successive acts of reflection.

How does Locke's theory account for knowledge of kind? In order to answer this question, consider the knowledge that you now have before you a *book*. We assume that you have already read Chapter 13 of *Lovers of Wisdom*. Thus, at some time, call it T1, you had a perception of *Lovers of Wisdom*. This perception was then stored in your memory. Later, you picked up *this* book, at some time T2. At T2, then, you had another perception of a book. This perception was also stored in memory. Then, these two stored perceptions were abstracted from your memory to create a new, abstract idea. This new abstract idea consists of the features common to these two perceptions. We might think of this abstract idea as the essence of a book, that which is common to all an only books. Now, with this new abstract idea in your head, you are able to judge whether further objects possess bookhood. You do this by comparing your abstract idea with new perceptions. If they sufficiently match, then the new item is of that kind; it is a book.

So, briefly and in general, we start out with an idea (of some object) in perception. An idea is passively presented to the mind (the blank slate). We then store a copy of this idea in memory. Call this idea "I1." Eventually, we encounter *another* particular object and our senses provide us with a new idea. Once again, we store a copy in memory. Call this new idea "I2." We now have ideas I1 and I2 The mind then takes what is common to these two ideas, and constructs a new *abstract* idea. It is called "abstract," because it was created by a process of abstraction. The mind abstracted from I1 and I2 what is common to both. It then saved this new image. Call this abstract idea "A1." Again, it consist of what I1 and I2 have in common. As we encounter different particular objects, new ideas are created. And if these ideas resemble A1, then the mind recognizes the new ideas as an A1. More accurately, the recognizes the objects represented by the new ideas as A1's. They are perceived as belonging to the *kind* A1. In sum, we start with particular objects, and form particular ideas of them (ideas). From these particular ideas we abstract to create abstract ideas. The abstract idea serves as a representative of all particulars of a certain kind. Whenever an idea resembles A1, we recognize it as belonging to the kind A1. In this way Locke attempts to account for knowledge of kind without appealing to innate ideas.

Exercise

1.   **The Test**: Determine whether Locke's account is successful. How? Find yourself a blank slate, and a set of sense organs (several sheets of paper, and a pen will do).[52]   You will

---

[52]For the sake of simplicity we will pretend that our only sense organs are our eyes. And remember, you are the blank slate. Try not to use any of the knowledge that came with you to this experiment. Shelve it until after the exercise.

also need two objects of the same kind (e.g., two cups, two pieces of chalk, etc.). Now, place one of these objects in front of you, and perform the following steps:

> **Step 1 (Receive Simple Impression):** Glance in the direction of the object. Now without giving special attention to any particular feature of the observation, impress on your slate the very simple ideas in your visual field. That is, represent the observed shape, and color of the object in front of you, by drawing these features using the conventions specified below.

Be careful not to represent any two simple ideas (say, of red and rectangularity) as one idea. Remember, "... the ideas ... enter by sense simple and unmixed."[53] The red idea and the rectangularity idea are received unmixed in the same way that a person blind his whole life, after finally gaining his sight, must learn to coordinate the unfamiliar visual images and the familiar tactile images into one perception.

Conventions for Representing Simple Ideas

> Use the following set of conventions to represent impressions on your blank slate.[54]

> Represent **shapes** with lined figures -- for example,

$$\square \quad , \quad \bigcirc \quad , \quad \text{and} \quad \triangle \quad .$$

> Represent **colors** with blotches containing the name of the color -- for example,

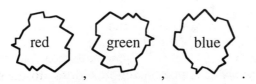

> **Step 2 (Store and Reflect):** Now that the simple ideas have been impressed, the "internal sense" can go to work. On the same slate, compound your simple ideas together to make complex ideas. That is, manipulate with your internal sense (your pen) the simple ideas by overlapping and conjoining them in virtually every combination that you can think of.

Next, take your second object, and place it front of you. Store your ideas in memory (i.e., set your full sheet aside). Take out a clean sheet of paper (clean the slate).

> **Step 3:** Repeat Step 1 and Step 2.

> **Step 4 (Compare):** Recall all the ideas stored in memory (i.e., the figures on your first sheet), and check to see if any of these complex ideas, match up with the complex ideas on the new slate.

---

[53] Locke's *Essay Concerning Human Understanding*, p. 15.
[54] Also for simplicity, we will reduce the number of possible kinds of simple impressions.

If any such complex ideas match up or resemble each other, then *recognition* has occurred. That is, if some complex idea from memory matches up with some other complex idea currently on the slate, then -- from the perspective of the cognizer -- the new idea is seen as a particular *kind* of thing. So, the recognizing of some idea as the same kind, is just the "matching up" of the two ideas.

If such recognition of kind can be acquired by the above method (via steps 1-4), and if the above method is a good model of Locke's theory of knowledge acquisition, then it seems that Locke has accomplished half of what he intended to accomplish. He has explained without an appeal to innate ideas, how one can be aware of the kind of thing that something is. In other words, he has explained how one comes to perceive objects *as* objects of certain kinds despite the fact that the senses alone give us perceptions only (not perception *as*).

Summary of procedure:

Step 1: **Receive** Simple Impressions
Step 2: **Store** and **Reflect**
Step 3: **Repeat** steps 1 and 2
Step 4: **Compare** Ideas

A Lockean Account of Knowledge of Identity?

Now let's see if Locke's theory can account for knowledge of identity (recognition of an object as one and the same object over time). Store your complex ideas from the last observation (Step 3 above) in memory (i.e., put your second sheet with the first). Take out a clean sheet of paper (clean the slate). Without altering the conditions from the last observation, go on to the next step.

Step 5: Repeat Steps 1 and 2.

Since we have not changed a thing, just recopy the complex ideas from your second sheet (or imagine that you have so re-impressed them).

Step 6 (Compare): Recall all the complex ideas stored in memory, and check to see if any complex ideas there match up *perfectly* with any complex ideas on the slate.

Suppose that two such complex ideas do match up perfectly. Has the cognizer *recognized* an object as one and the same object at two different times? According to Locke, Yes. The new idea, Locke would say, is seen as the *same* thing as previously observed. It is seen as one and the same thing that it matches up with from memory. The recognizing of some idea as perfectly identical to another just is the perfect matching of two ideas.

If recognition of sameness can be acquired by the above method (via steps 1 - 6), with the additional of the other senses and their respective simple ideas, and if the resulting method is a good model of Locke's theory of knowledge acquisition, then Locke has not only explained knowledge of kind, but he has explained knowledge of identity. Locke alleges to explain our knowledge without a commitment to the existence of innate ideas. If he has done so, then -- by the principle of Ockham's Razor -- Locke's theory wins out over Descartes'.

Exercise

2. Assume that the above procedure accurately represents Locke's theory of knowledge acquisition. Decide whether Locke can in fact account for knowledge of kind and sameness (via the above procedure). Defend your answer.

Chapter 14

Berkeley

The Death of the Material World

As John Locke took Ockham's Razor to Descartes' theory of knowledge, so Berkeley turns the razor in on Locke.[55] Recall Locke's distinction between primary and secondary qualities. What is the difference between a primary and a secondary quality? Locke tells us that what distinguishes primary from secondary qualities is the *kind* of substance in which these qualities inhere. Primary qualities (such as shape, quantity, and motion) inhere in extended, unthinking (i.e., material) substance, and secondary qualities (such as colors, tastes, and sounds) inhere in thinking, unextended (i.e., mental) substance. The primary qualities out in the world somehow bring about secondary qualities in us. So, on Locke's view, qualities like shape, quantity and motion out there, causes colors, tastes and sounds in us. The material world that realizes these primary properties, then, is the basic stuff of which the objective world consists. It is the source of all knowledge. That world is the world that our knowledge is about. The *material* world. Berkeley, however, denies the existence of this material stuff. In effect, he takes Ockham's Razor and slashes Locke's theory and the material world to death.

But, a few more things get caught in the crossfire. In rejecting the reality of material substance, Berkeley consequently rejects the distinction between primary and secondary qualities. Furthermore, Berkeley denies that there are two kinds of ideas, particular and abstract. Abstract ideas, upon which Locke's theory of knowledge heavily depended, he claims, are impossible. At the end of this chapter, we review one reason why Berkeley believes this. It will do for now to note that Berkeley alleges to do all the work that Locke attempted to do (that is, explain the acquisition of all our knowledge), but without the need for abstract ideas. In other words, Berkeley's offer is of an equally good theory, but one that requires the positing of fewer distinct kinds of things. Remember Ockham's Razor: "Do not multiply entities beyond necessity."

An *ontology* (a theory about what kinds of things exist) can be thought of as a list of entities. Notice that compared to Locke's, Berkeley's ontology is small. Locke has a very big ontology.

Locke's Ontology	Berkeley's Ontology
Mental Substance	Mental Substance
Material Substance	Secondary Qualities
Primary Qualities	Particular Ideas
Secondary Qualities	
Particular Ideas	
Abstract Ideas	

Berkeley's argument for the non-existence of the material follows from considerations about language. He takes the term 'material substance' to be meaningless. The important

---

[55]For detailed discussion of Ockham's Razor see the Appendix to Chapter 7 above, and §7.3 of *Lovers of Wisdom*.

question, then, is this: why does Berkeley take the term 'material substance' to have no meaning? More specifically, this question becomes the following: why does he think that there is nothing to which those words refer (nothing real that they designate)? Berkeley's answer seems to be that (1) a word (or phrase) does not mean anything on its own; it needs an idea associated with it, and (2) no idea is associated with the phrase 'material substance.' If Berkeley is correct on this score, then the phrase 'material substance' is meaningless, and so refers to nothing. We will most of this chapter trying to make clear the steps of the above argument; (1) concerning reference and meaning, and (2) concerning the phrase 'material substance.'

Meaning and Reference

An ant crawls through the sand leaving a thin path in its wake. Entirely by chance, it inscribes what we would take to be the sentence "The Sun is eternal." The ant, of course, does not know English. That the ant scribbled what it did was a coincidence, a complete and utter fluke. In this case, do we want to say that the ant referred to the Sun? Were its markings in the sand meaningful? Were they *about* anything at all?[56]

Your ear suddenly catches a voice spoken in a foreign language. Maybe it is Serbo-Croatian, or maybe Russian. You are not quite sure, but you do remember one catchy phrase that was uttered. It was pronounced "boga-sa-ya-yay." You start thinking the sounds to yourself and speaking them out loud. The question is, are you really thinking *about* or saying anything at all? Do these "words" refer to anything when you imitate them? Do the mental images and sounds that you conjure up "hook onto the world?" Remember, you do not understand the sounds, you simply mimic them.

The purpose of these two thought-experiments is to convince you that pieces of language do not acquire their meanings all by themselves. It is not just the sounds and inkblots that make them refer to what they do. To put it another way, some words refer to things in the world (for example, the word 'Sun' refers to the luminous celestial body around which the earth orbits). And it is not in virtue of features found in the string of symbols 'Sun' that makes that string refer to what it refers to (namely, the said celestial body). Language does not connect up with the world on its own. More is needed to fix reference.

What we want you to see in the above two scenarios is that both you and the ant put forth some piece of language, yet neither of you refer, depict or represent anything at all in those cases. The ant's inscriptions and your mimicking are not about anything, any more than accidentally spilled paint that coincidentally lands in the form of a perfectly painted tree is a picture *of* a tree. A word's referent is not determined solely by the order of the symbols -- that is, it is not determined solely by the syntax.

If reference issued from features of the word in isolation, then one could take the word 'Sun' in isolation from the world, the context, the history of the word's use, its conceptual relations to others fragments of the language, etc. and still be able to determine what it refers to. But we can do this no more with 'Sun' than with foreign words that we do not already understand (such as, maybe, 'Schnee' or 'pluie'). As it stands, 'Sun,' as with any word that can represent something, does not depict something in the world merely in virtue of features had by the string of symbols 'S,' 'u,' 'n.'

Such considerations motivate the need for a theory of meaning, an account of the nature of meanings. But what are meanings? For Locke, Berkeley, and even Hume (whom you will meet in the next chapter) the answer is "an idea."[57] Reference is fixed not only by a fragment of language, say, a word, but by the idea associated with the word. 'Sun,' then, refers to the Sun because we have the relevant idea of the Sun associated with our uses of 'Sun.' The ant that etches those markings in the sand does not refer to anything, on this view,

---

[56]Hilary Putnam provides a similar thought experiment and discusses similar considerations about meaning in *Reasons Truth and History*, (Cambridge, 1981).

[57]It was not until Kant (Chapter 16) that an alternative to ideas was offered as the basic components of meaning. Kant discussed the need for concepts and rules as further building blocks of meaning. And it was not until the language philosophers (Chapter 22) that it was argued that meanings "just ain't in the head" at all.

because the ant does not have any meaning (idea) associated with its scribbles. When you think to yourself of a foreign phrase that you do not grasp, you do not mean anything. So you cannot refer. By Berkeley's lights, a fragment of language (utterance or inkblot) can have meaning (and so can designate something real) only if an idea is associated with that fragment by the person entertaining it.

"Material Substance"

Empiricist's believe that, like our knowledge of the world, the meanings of our words have experience as their source. We start with our ideas in perception, associate with these ideas sounds and inkblots (strings of symbols), and in this empirical way we construct for ourselves all of the meanings of all our words and sentences. For instance, we learned the meaning of 'ball' by being presented with a ball while mother uttered "ball!" several dozen times. Soon thereafter, we understood (i.e., grasped the meaning of) the word 'ball.' We became able to recall our stored idea of a ball when presented with the term 'ball.' Similarly, we learned the word 'snow' by experience. More complex terms such as 'snowball' we learned in a derivative way by combining in experience the simple terms 'snow' and 'ball,' and annexing them to the single term 'snowball.' For the empiricists, we acquire a grasp of the meanings of all terms in this "bottom-up" fashion, that is by first grasping the meanings of simple terms, and then building up meaningful complex terms out of the simples.

Now the empiricist John Locke believed in material substance. But much to our epistemological dismay, he wrote, we cannot know what such material substance consists in. He says,

> ... if anyone will examine himself concerning his notion of pure
> substance in general, he will find he has no other idea of it at all,
> but only a supposition of he knows not what support of such
> qualities which are capable of producing simple ideas in us...[58]

In other words, we have not a single idea as to what the underlying material substance is like, for we only have direct acquaintance with our own ideas, secondary qualities. Our ideas of primary qualities, at best, *represent* primary qualities accurately. We do not directly apprehend them, and consequently, cannot directly grasp the substance in which they inhere. Berkeley then argues that since we cannot grasp such material substance, the phrase 'material substance' cannot refer to anything real. In fact, the phrase 'material substance,' according to Berkeley, is nothing but a series of inkblots! That is what he means when he says that "there is no distinct meaning annexed to [these words]." What do we mean when we hear or utter the phrase 'material substance'? Nothing at all! Locke failed to notice this consequence of his very own theory. There lies the tension in Locke's theory; he advocated the existence of primary, material substance, while denying that our words could refer past the possibility of experience. Berkeley made explicit this tension in Locke's empiricism, and resolved it.[59] This is yet another example of rational criticism. Berkeley took the first step of rational criticism when he made explicit a crucial flaw in Locke's theory of knowledge. He did this by making a simple observation -- namely, that we have no idea of that which is beyond all ideas. He took the second step of rational criticism by constructing his own theory.

The upshot is that no matter how much combining and deriving of meanings one does, one cannot refer to something beyond the possibility of experience. From experience all meaning is derived, so ultimately all reference points back to it. We cannot get outside our own picture of the world. Material substance, however, *is* outside of it all. Therefore, by 'material substance' we "know not what" we mean, and so mean nothing at all.

---

[58]Locke, *An Essay Concerning Human Understanding*: Bk.II, chap. XXIII, sec. 2.
[59]Be aware that David Hume in the next chapter (Chapter 15) takes this line even further by denying the existence of mental substance. As we will see, without mental substance one's own identity is uncertain, contrary to the conclusion arrived at by Descartes in *Meditation II* (chapter 10).

Summarizing a Berkelean Argument

In summary, then, one of Berkeley's arguments that material substance does not exist is this:

So,
(i) Terms do not mean things on their own.   [defended at the start of the chapter]

(ii) a term is meaningful if and only if it is associated with an idea.   [principle of idea theory motivated by (i)]

Now,
(iii) all ideas are acquired in experience,   [principle of empiricism]

and
(iv) there is no experience of material substance.   [as Locke pointed out for Berkeley]

So,
(v) we have no idea of material substance.   [from (iii) and (iv)]

But then
(vi) the term 'material substance' is meaningless.   [from (ii) and (v)]

Therefore,
(vii) 'material substance' refers to no existing thing.   [from (vi)]

In this way, Berkeley argues that the primary stuff of which reality is made is not material. What remains as the basic substance of the world is the mental. Everything that exists, inheres in mind. From Descartes we learned that minds are essentially thinking and perceiving things. To inhere in a mind, then, is to be thought or perceived. And so goes the Berkelean slogan: to be is to be perceived!

Abstract versus Particular Ideas

Recall Locke's theory of abstract ideas. Such ideas, claimed Locke, are generated from particular ideas associated with particular objects that have some cluster of properties in common. Unfortunately, Locke's theory of abstract ideas is in tension with empiricism -- the very position that Locke endorses. As Berkeley pointed out, abstract ideas are not perceived, though Locke contends otherwise. Since abstract ideas do not include that which is particular to each idea (e.g., the abstract idea of "bookhood" does not include that which is particular to each idea that is associated with a particular book), we are left with no perceivable idea. For instance, as Locke mentions we may "...leave out of the complex idea we have of Peter and James and Mary and Jane that which is peculiar to each, and retain only what is common to them all." Such an abstraction would form the general idea referred to by the word 'person.' But Berkeley, and Hume later, note that nothing perceivable would be left to form such an abstracted general idea. The abstract idea would depict a person neither male nor female, large or small, standing or sitting, light skinned or dark. All features not shared by each person would be put aside in the abstraction process. What would be left? According to Berkeley, nothing.

Berkeley attempted to resolve this difficulty by explaining that general ideas are particular in nature and are not abstract. This means that the general ideas of say "book" and "person," by which we respectively represent all books and people to ourselves, do not abandon all characteristics that are particular to only some books and people. Rather, according to Berkeley, such ideas are of particular books and particular persons, and so have some idiosyncratic characteristics. But even though particular ideas are particular and are not general, they nevertheless function to stand for everything of a certain kind. For Berkeley and Hume, the job of a general idea remains the same. A general idea acts as a *representative* of all particulars of a given kind. Only in this sense are they general. And such representative ideas are not necessarily void of everything idiosyncratic to any one of them. Quite the contrary. They must be particular in nature to be perceived at all.

By characterizing abstract (general) ideas in this way, Berkeley has taken the second step of rational criticism. He has modified Locke's account of knowledge acquisition in order to avoid its latent difficulties. He has offered a positive solution to the tension in Locke's theory. In doing so he has offered a better characterization of how it is that knowledge is possible.

Chapter 15

Hume

The Death of the Self

Recall the problem of knowledge raised by Descartes, and then by Locke and Berkeley after him.[60] The problem was of explaining how it is that we acquire knowledge of the world despite the fact that we are directly acquainted only with our own mental states. In previous sections we concentrated on two kinds of knowledge, knowledge of identity (the continued existence of an object over time) and knowledge of kind (the sort of thing an object is, e.g. a book, or piece of wax, etc.). To explain how we acquire these types of knowledge, Descartes availed himself of innate ideas. Locke, wielding Ockham's Razor, offered an explanation using no innate ideas, involving only particular and abstract ideas. His theory did involve the mention of material substance (the ultimate stuff of which he supposed the world around us is made) and mental substance (a "tabula rasa," or blank slate, on which ideas appear, the stuff of which the mind ultimately consists). Berkeley as well swung Ockham's Razor, but into Locke's theory. Berkeley revised Locke's theory of knowledge by eliminating the need for material substance, hence his idealism. Hume goes even further in slicing Locke's theory. He eliminates the need for mental substance. So he adopts Berkeley's modifications of Locke's account, but goes a step farther by slashing the concept of self to its death.

Three Empiricist Ontologies

Locke's Ontology	Berkeley's Ontology	Hume's Ontology
Ideas	Ideas	Ideas
Mental Substance	Mental Substance	
Material Substance		

Hume takes empiricism to its logical conclusion by denying the legitimacy of the self. Positing a simple unchanging stuff in which all perceptions inhere (an underlying reality that makes you the same person over time), he argues, is unjustified. Hume abolishes the need for the traditional notion of personal identity. He denies his own personal identity, and suggests that you do the same. What is his argument? We will discuss it and present to you an exercise in logic to determine the alternative consequences of his argument. But first, how exactly does Hume believe that we acquire knowledge, particularly, knowledge of the identity (continued existence) and of objects generally? Answering this latter question will shed light on why Hume takes a belief in personal identity to be unwarranted.

Does the Word "I" Mean Anything?

For an idea theorist, the meaningfulness, and so, the reference, of a term is dependent upon the idea associated with that term. If there is no idea corresponding to a particular term, the term is meaningless (and so, has no referent). The most developed idea theory of this sort

---

[60]Of course, nearly every philosopher from Thales, Anaximander and Anaximenes (the earliest philosophers considered in *Lovers of Wisdom*) up to Descartes and beyond, in one form or another, has considered these questions.

is found in Hume, though its origin is found in Locke. Hume refines Locke's theory to handle various problems raised by Locke's critics. What Locke called "perceptions," Hume calls "impressions," and he calls any object of awareness that is not an impression an "idea." Memories and afterimages are examples of Humean ideas. Hume tells us, very much in the spirit of Locke, that "We never can conceive any thing but perceptions [that is, impressions or ideas]...."

Now Descartes tells us that there is one thing that you cannot doubt -- namely, your own existence. For in doubting at all you must be there to do the doubting. Even if this is all a dream and even if the hands you see before you are not real, there is nonetheless someone doing the dreaming. Even if all your experiences are implanted by an evil demon whose sole task is to deceive you, there must be someone there being deceived. In sum, we might be wrong about virtually everything. All your beliefs might be false; all except one -- namely, your belief that you exist. If you have the belief, its truth cannot be coherently doubted by you. That's what Descartes told us.

Many of us believe that we do exist, that we each have a personal identity. Personal identity is considered by the philosophers we are presently discussing to be the continued existence of some simple and unchanging thing (some underlying stuff) that makes you the same person over time. Hume asks whether we have an idea of the self as a numerically identical entity over time. If so, then there must be some impression of which this idea is a representation. But, according to Hume, there is no such impression. And so, there is no referent of 'I,' the word 'I' is meaningless, the self doesn't exist, and Descartes was wrong all along.

Many of us believe that cause and effect exist in the world. Many of us believe that God exists, or, with Descartes, that we exist as one and the same individual over time. We believe that we have a personal identity. As you probably noticed from reading *Lovers of Wisdom*, Hume takes all of these things to be fictitious. He argues that since we have no impression or idea of these things, our words that are supposed to designate them are meaningless. Therefore those words do not refer to anything. Causation, God and persons do not exist in the objective, mind-independent world. It does not even make sense to say that they do, on this view, since 'causation,' 'God,' and 'persons' are meaningless terms. Don't many of us *believe* that these things exist, and don't we believe that they exist because we are in a position to know that they exist? Hume argues that without the appropriate ideas, we are not in a position to know such things. So why, then, do so many of us believe that causation, God and persons exist? Hume tries to answer this question.

Why Do We Believe We Exist?

Hume notes that the senses alone and unassisted are not sufficient to account for the attribution of sameness over time. He calls such attributing "believing the continued existence" of an object. So, for Hume, seeming to perceive some X at a time T2 as the same X as previously perceived at some earlier time T1 is to have a belief that X has a continued existence.

Hume recognizes that images (ideas or impressions) are not sufficient to give rise to the belief in continued existence for the following reasons: (i) all perceptions are new and distinct and fleeting with regard to their existence; they do not have a continued existence. Such a fleeting existence of a perception is not sufficient to convey the idea of a continually existing object, and (ii) nothing about a single perception that is immediately presented by the senses conveys the notion of a continued existence of an object. Hume notes that there is never a perception of sameness but only perceptions of figure, bulk, motion, solidity, color, tastes, smells, sounds, heat, cold, pains or pleasures. Since fleeting perceptions are not sufficient to produce the belief in continued existence, Hume accounts for the production of this belief with what he calls "the imagination." So the question becomes, "how is it that the imagination enables us to believe in the continued existence of objects among discontinuing perceptions?"[61]

---

[61]Immanuel Kant (Chapter 16) tries to answer this question after Hume. He also attempts to clarify the role of the imagination in acquiring knowledge of the world.

Belief in general, he states, "consists in nothing but the vivacity of an idea." So, we look at a table in front of us, and then close our eyes. The memory presents a fairly strong idea of that table, and the imagination produces a "vivacity" on that idea of the table. This vivacity of the idea, "table," makes us believe that the table continues to exist. This belief that the table continues to exist is fictitious, for Hume, because what we are believing to exist over time (an idea of the table) is actually fleeting.

We leave the room and come back. We have a new sense impression of a table at this time, T2. Due to the resemblance of this table to our former idea of the table (which occurred at T1), which the memory bestows also at T2, the imagination imparts a vivacity on our new sense impression causing us to believe that it is the *same* table -- that is, causing us to believe that our table at T2 has a continued existence. On Hume's view, in this case, the belief of a continued existence is a fiction, because the existence of the new sense impression is really new, distinct, and has a discontinuous existence.

Hume has uncovered a puzzle which he admits he cannot solve. The problem is to explain how the imagination can attribute a continued existence to objects (for example, persons) based on the discontinuous existence of impressions and ideas. Such mental images have no continued existence, or at least, have not a very long-lived existence, while we attribute a continued existence to the objects these images represent. Hume explains that any account of how we come to attribute identity to things must not ignore this tension, it must resolve it. So how is it that we instinctively and uncontrollably attribute a continued existence to objects, though on careful philosophical analysis (we are told) we realize that there is no perception of this continued existence (identity over time)?

Hume left this puzzle for other philosophers to mull over. Immanuel Kant (Chapter 16), for instance, tells us that he was "woken from his dogmatic slumber" in search of a solution. One good philosophy paper would be to explain how Kant attempts to solve this problem. The above considerations have put us in a position to understand how Hume kills the self.

Logic and Personal Identity

When a set of assumptions leads to a contradiction, what dialectical moves are we licensed to make? A contradiction is a conjunction composed of a sentence P and its negation not-P. For instance, "All whales are mammals, and not all whales are mammals" or "2+2=4, but 2+2≠4" are contradictions. Such propositions are generally understood as necessarily false. Now, let's suppose that a contradiction logically follows from some assumption A. What are we as rational beings obliged to accept or reject at this point? We are, of course, obliged to reject the contradiction since a contradiction is always false. But the contradiction rests on our assumption A -- that is, it follows logically from the truth of A. So, we are obliged to reject the assumption A as well. Not-A, then, follows from a contradiction that rests on the assumption A. For example, assume that Smith robbed the bank. It follows then that Smith was at the bank at the time of the crime. But Smith was at the charity convention when the robbery occurred. Then Smith *wasn't* at the bank when the robbery occurred. So, Smith was at the bank at the time of the robbery and he was not at the bank at the time of the robbery. Contradiction! Therefore, Smith did not rob the bank. Notice that there is more than one assumption at play here. There is the assumption that Smith robbed the bank, and there is also the assumption that Smith was in fact at the charity convention. When faced with a contradiction, all else being equal, one is licensed to reject ANY assumption supporting that contradiction. On the other hand, if we have independent reasons for not rejecting certain assumptions, then our choices are narrowed down. If we all saw and spoke with Smith at the charity convention, then our only choice, it seems, is to reject the claim that Smith robbed the bank. The logical strategy of deriving a contradiction from a set of assumptions in order to reject one of those assumptions is called *reductio ad absurdum* (reduction to absurdity).

Hume's personal identity argument takes the form of a *reductio*. Suppose that all the logical moves of the argument are licit, that the argument is valid.[62] In other words, let's grant

---

[62]For a detailed discussion of validity and other logical notions, see Chapter 7 above.

that there has been no logical error at any step of the argument.[63] But there is still room to argue with Hume. You may disagree with him on which assumption to negate in light of the contradiction. And if you can find no grounds to negate the appropriate assumption, it could mean the death of you.

Exercise

Decide whether you agree with Hume's choice of conclusion (following the contradiction), and defend your position. Notice that if you block the move to line 7, you cannot derive the ultimate conclusion at line 9. Here's Hume's argument:

(1) We are aware of (have knowledge of) our own personal identity (our simple, unchanging, continuous self).
[**Assumption** from common sense]

(2) We are directly aware of nothing but our own ideas.
[**Assumption** of Empiricism]

So,

(3) we have an idea of personal identity (of a simple, unchanging, continuous self).
[From 1 and 2]

(4) Every ideas must resemble some impression (namely, the one from which the idea was derived).[64]
[**Assumption** of Hume's empiricism]

Then,

(5) there is some simple, unchanging and continuous impression (of the self).
[From 3 and 4]

But,

(6) there is no such simple, unchanging and continuous impression (anywhere in experience).
[**Assumption** from introspection]

CONTRADICTION!

Therefore,

(7) we are not aware of our own personal identity.
[By **reductio**]

Furthermore,

(8) If we can reasonably attribute personal identity to ourselves, then we must be aware of our personal identity.
[**Assumption** from empiricism]

Hence,

(9) we cannot reasonably attribute personal identity to ourselves.
[From 7 and 8]

---

[63]Notice, though, your sense of uneasiness moving so quickly from premises 3 and 4 to the conclusion at 5.
[64]For empiricists like Hume "inference to the best explanation" was not the prominent and decisive philosophical strategy for deciding which things exist (as it sometimes is today). Rather, he embraced the notion that what we are allowed to countenance are things that can be understood in terms of the stuff that we already know to exist. For example, atoms can be intelligibly countenanced, according to this principle, just as long as they behave like our medium sized objects such as tables, chairs, billiard balls, etc.

Chapter 16

Kant

Kant's philosophy, perhaps more so than any other in *Lovers of Wisdom*, is a massive web of concepts and distinctions that are tightly spun together with a peculiar terminology. One might say that Kant invented his own language in order to better understand the activities of the human mind. Of course, in order to appreciate Kant's insights, one must understand both the distinctions that Kant makes, and the terminology that he uses to mark them. So, in this chapter we will make these distinctions and clarify the Kantian terminology. This should not only deepen your understanding of Kant, but will also help you to master a powerful framework that was used to clarify both the nature of mind, and the relationship between mind and reality.

In the first section we will distinguish analytic and synthetic judgments, and in the second we will distinguish *apriori* and *aposteriori* judgments. This will allow us to understand what Kant takes to be the central *question* of all of metaphysics: how is synthetic *apriori* knowledge possible? Then, in the third section, we will distinguish the phenomenal from the noumenal world, and in the fourth we will distinguish three faculties of the mind: intuition, understanding, and reason. This will allow us to understand Kant's *answer* to the central question of all metaphysics.

The Analytic/Synthetic Distinction

The terms 'analytic' and 'synthetic' refer to different types of *judgment*. The difference between these judgments regards a difference in the relation between subject and predicate: in an analytic judgment the predicate is part of the very concept of the subject, while in a synthetic judgment the predicate is not part of the concept of the subject.

Consider these two judgments:

(i) The Sun is a star.
(ii) The Sun is about five billion years old.

(i) is analytic, and (ii) is synthetic. Why? Recall our earlier discussion of predicates in Chapter 2. Roughly, the subject of a sentence is what the sentence is *about*, while the predicate is what the sentence says about that subject. The above two judgments are about the Sun; the one says it is a star and the other says it is about five billion years old. Thus, in those two judgments, 'the Sun' is the subject, and 'is a star' and 'is about five billion years old' are the respective predicates. But (i) is analytic since the concept of the Sun (the very meaning of the word 'Sun') informs us that it is a star. (ii), on the other hand, is synthetic since the concept of the Sun does *not* inform us that the Sun is about five billion years old.

One important point which we can note here is that a synthetic judgment, unlike an analytic one, can be false. For, the concept of the Sun does not inform us, say, that the Sun is ten feet in diameter. So the judgment "the Sun is ten feet in diameter" is synthetic. But, no experience, experiment, or measurement at all informs us that the Sun is ten feet in diameter. In fact, we are informed to the contrary, that the Sun is 864,000 miles in diameter. So, the judgment "the Sun is ten feet in diameter," in addition to being synthetic, is false (and is made false by some feature of the Sun, namely its diameter).

So, in order to determine whether a judgment is analytic or synthetic, one should consider the relationship between the subject and the predicate of that judgment. But what about this relationship should one consider? What is it about the relationship between 'the

Sun' and 'is a star' that makes the judgment "the Sun is a star" analytic? And what is it about the relationship between 'the Sun' and 'is about five billion years old' that makes the judgment "the Sun is about five billion years old" synthetic? Kant tells us that

> ...Analytic judgments express nothing in the predicate but what has been already actually thought in the concept of the subject...On the other hand, [a synthetic judgment] contains in its predicate something not actually thought [in the concept of the subject].[65]

Think of the word which names the subject of a judgment. If you know the meaning of this word, ask yourself, "does the meaning of this word inform me that this judgment is true?" If so, the judgment is analytic. If not, the judgment is synthetic.

Thus, the difference between analytic and synthetic judgments is a difference in the nature of the relationship between the subject and predicate of those judgments. Either the predicate is part of the concept of the subject or it is not. If it is, the judgment is analytic. If it is not, the judgment is synthetic.[66]

From the above discussion, we can make the following observation about analytic and synthetic judgments (and this observation is crucial to understanding synthetic *apriori* knowledge). Consider a judgment which is true. Then ask *why* is it true? If the judgment is true in virtue of the concepts (or the meaning of the words) in it, it is analytic. If the judgment is true in virtue of some feature of the object it is about, it is synthetic. For example, the judgment "the Sun is a star" is true because the meaning of the word 'Sun' includes the information that the Sun is a star. Thus, that judgment is analytic. On the other hand, the judgment "the Sun is about five billion years old" is true not because of the meaning of the words 'Sun,' or 'is,' or 'five billion years old,' but because of a certain feature of the Sun, namely its age. Thus, this judgment is synthetic.

Therefore, if you know whether some judgment is analytic or synthetic, then you know something about the relation between the subject and the predicate of the judgment (whether the predicate is or is not part of the concept of the subject). But, if you know whether some (true) judgment is analytic or synthetic, you also know something about why it is true. You know that in virtue of which it is true. An analytic judgment is true in virtue of the concepts (meaning), and a synthetic judgment (when true) is true in virtue of objects (the world).[67]

---

[65]From *Prolegomena to Any Future Metaphysics*, translation revised by James W. Ellington from Carus. Hackett. 1977. Indianapolis.

[66]One important consequence of the relation between subject and predicate in analytic judgments is that the denial of an analytic judgment is a contradiction. (The denial of a synthetic judgment, on the other hand, is not.) For, if the judgment is analytic, then the predicate is part of the concept of the subject of the judgment. To deny such a judgment is thus equivalent to saying that one and the same predicate is both true and false of the same subject (at the same time); a contradiction.

[67]For a technical correction which may take us slightly further into detail than necessary for this general overview, see the appendix at the end of this chapter.

Analytic	Synthetic
Judgments based on meaning *(concepts)*	Judgments based on the world *(objects)*

Division of Judgments According to What Makes Them True

Exercise

1. Think of your own examples of two analytic and two (true) synthetic judgments.

Analytic Judgments
(i) _____
(ii) _____

Synthetic Judgments
(i) _____
(ii) _____

The Apriori/Aposteriori Distinction

The terms *'apriori'* and *'aposteriori'* also refer to types of judgments. But, whereas the difference between analytic and synthetic judgments is based on *what makes them true* (or false), the difference between *apriori* and *aposteriori* judgments is based on *how we know that they are true* (or false). As Kant explains:

> ...*apriori* knowledge [is] not knowledge independent of this or that experience, but knowledge absolutely independent of all experience. Opposed to it is empirical knowledge, which is knowledge possible only *aposteriori*, that is, through experience.[68]

It is important to note that by 'independent of all experience' Kant does not mean *prior* to all experience. *Apriori* knowledge is not the same as 'innate knowledge.' To make this clear Kant writes, "There can be no doubt that all our knowledge begins with experience...But though all our knowledge begins with experience, it does not follow that it all arises out of experience." [69] Thus, *apriori* knowledge is not knowledge had prior to any experience (i.e. before birth). Rather, *apriori* knowledge does not require any experience, *so long as one understands the concepts involved in the judgment.* So, to say that the judgment 'all bachelors are unmarried men' is known *apriori* is not to say that one could know this if one had no experience whatsoever. Rather, it is to say that once we understand the meaning of 'bachelor' and 'unmarried male,' one knows that this judgment is true without needing to appeal to experience. One does not have to survey a sample of bachelors in order to determine whether 'all bachelors are unmarried men' is true. Rather, one only needs to understand the meaning of 'bachelor' and of 'unmarried male.' Mathematical claims are also apriori on this view. They are so, because one need not appeal to experience in order to know them.

---

[68]From *Critique of Pure Reason*, trns. Norman Kemp Smith. Page 43 (B2-B3). St. Martin's Press. New York. 1965.
[69]*Critique of Pure Reason*, B1.

Aposteriori knowledge, on the other hand, is knowledge which must be acquired through experience. For instance, "grass is green," and "there is a book in front of you." All of your perceptual beliefs is *aposteriori*.

JUDGMENTS

apriori	aposteriori
Judgments known *independently of experience*	Judgments known *through experience*

Division of Judgments According to How We Know They Are True

Exercise

2.   Think of your own examples of two *apriori* judgments and two *aposteriori* judgments.

Apriori Judgments
(i) _____
(ii) _____

Aposteriori Judgments
(i) _____
(ii) _____

If we divide the class of judgments according to *both* of these distinctions (the analytic/synthetic and the *apriori/aposteriori* distinctions), we can distinguish four kinds of judgments:

Judgments

	analytic	synthetic
apriori	Judgments made true *by concepts* and known *independently of experience*	Judgments made true *by objects* and known *independently of experience*
aposteriori	Judgments made true *by concepts* and known *through experience*	judgments made true *by objects* and known *through experience*

Classification of Judgments According to What Makes Them True and How We Know Them to be True[70]

Exercise

3.   In order to become more fluent with this terminology, classify the following judgments according to the analytic/synthetic and *apriori/aposteriori* distinctions. A helpful strategy for classifying any given judgment below is this: (i) isolate the subject and the predicate in the judgment. Then, determine (ii) whether the judgment is analytic or synthetic, and (iii) whether the judgment is *apriori* or or *aposteriori*. (In order to determine whether the judgment is analytic or synthetic, ask yourself, "is the predicate part of the concept of the subject?"   In order to determine whether the judgment is *apriori* or *aposteriori*, ask yourself, "is this judgment knowable without perceptual experience, or is it only knowable only after experience?")

(a) Analytic apriori
(b) Analytic aposteriori
(c) Synthetic aposteriori
(d) Synthetic apriori

_____1. The Sun is a star.
_____2. Kant is the author of *The Critique of Pure Reason*.
_____3. All sisters are female.
_____4. The Earth moves around the Sun.
_____5. Every event has a cause.
_____6. J.S. Bach had twenty-one children.
_____7. All swans are white.
_____8. All swans are birds.
_____9. $397 \times 56 = 22,232$ (The sum of 397 and 56 is equal to 22,232.)
_____10. Gold has atomic number 79.
_____11. $E = Mc^2$ (Energy = mass $\times$ the speed of light^2)

---

[70]There are no analytic *a posteriori* truths, since a judgment made true by concepts is known to be true prior to any appeal to experience, and so will never be known from experience. Hence, that square is crossed out.

_____12. The judgment "All bachelors are unmarried men" is analytic *apriori*.[71]
_____13. [Your name] exists.
_____14. I exist.
_____15. π = 3.141592654...[72]

Next, think of your own examples:

Analytic apriori

1._____
2._____
3._____
4._____

Synthetic aposteriori

1._____
2._____
3._____
4._____

Synthetic apriori

1._____
2._____
3._____
4._____

Hopefully, you now have a clearer understanding of how Kant classified judgments. Analytic and synthetic judgments are classified according to the relationship between their subject and predicate; while *apriori* and aposteriori judgments are classified according to how we come to know whether they are true. Now we are ready to see what 'synthetic *apriori*' means, and with it, what is meant by the question 'how is synthetic *apriori* knowledge possible?'

Synthetic Apriori Knowledge

Let "S is P" be a synthetic judgment which you know *apriori*. Since you *know* "S is P," you know that the predicate P is true of the subject S. Since you know "S is P" *apriori*, you know it *independently of any experience* . But, since the judgment "S is P" is *synthetic*, it is not the case that P is simply part of the very concept of S. Thus, without an appeal to experience (of S or anything else), you know something about S which cannot be known by analyzing the concept of S. From both the exposition above, and from the material in *Lovers of Wisdom*, you know that synthetic *apriori* judgments are true in virtue of the way the world is (rather than the conceptual relationship between their subject and predicate), and yet are known independently of experience. But how can a judgment that is not merely conceptual -- that provides *information* about a subject that is not simply part of the concept of that subject -- be known independently of any experience? How can something about an *object* (and not merely about a concept, a meaning) be known without appealing to experience? The key to answering this lies in distinguishing the phenomenal from the noumenal world.

---

[71]Note: the *subject* of this judgment is 'The judgment "All bachelors are unmarried men"', (*not* 'all bachelors'), and the predicate is "is analytic *a priori*".
[72]Remember, π (Pi) is the ratio of the circumference to the diameter of a circle.

The Phenomenal/Noumenal Distinction

The terms we have examined so far ('analytic', 'synthetic', *'apriori'*, and *'aposteriori'*) distinguish *judgments* of different kinds. The terms 'phenomenal' and 'noumenal,' however, distinguish *objects* in two ways: objects as they are in experience are phenomenal objects, and objects as they are in themselves (independently of experience) are noumenal objects. The insight that a phenomenal object is *never* noumenal is Kant's way of saying that your eyes are not windows.

It is important to watch for the uses of the terms 'object' and 'things-in-themselves'. The term 'object' is sometimes used to mean objects of experience and, less frequently, to mean things in themselves. There are two modes of reality on Kant's view: phenomenal reality and noumenal reality. The mind is limited to constructing only phenomenal objects. The ambiguity of the term 'object' may have you thinking that Kant believed that the mind has a causal influence over things-in-themselves. He did not.[73] Rather, his view is that objects of experience -- phenomenal objects -- are constructed by certain mental faculties. Things-in-themselves, on the other hand, are *not* affected by the mind at all. It is only phenomenal reality that the mind actively constructs.

The Intuition/Understanding/Reason Distinction

Kant distinguishes phenomenal from noumenal objects in virtue of his insight that the mind is an active participant in the construction of the phenomenal reality -- the reality that we experience. But in what way is the mind an active participant in the construction of phenomena? Exactly what activities does the mind perform in the construction of phenomenal objects? Kant's answer is based on a distinction between three faculties of the mind: intuition, understanding, and reason. The mental activities of intuition, understanding, and reason, make experience -- and so phenomenal reality -- possible. Let's examine each of these activities in turn.

Intuition can be thought of as the activity of the mind that we sometimes call perception. But what exactly is involved in perception? Remember the distinction between *seeing* and *seeing as* that was discussed earlier (Chapter 5)? Let's apply this distinction to perception generally, thereby distinguishing *perceiving* and *perceiving as*. To illustrate, consider the following mark:

$$\exists$$

Surely you perceive the mark. But, unless you have studied quantification theory (first-order logic), you do not perceive this mark as an "existential quantifier." Perhaps you perceive it as a "backward E." In either case, you are perceiving the above mark *as* something. And when you perceive an entity as being of such-and-such a kind, you are imposing a *concept* on that entity. *Perceiving as* involves concepts. But the faculty of intuition does *not* involve concepts. Rather, the intuitive faculty creates perceptions without adding any conceptual interpretation to them. The intuition is the raw perceptual data.

Concepts are created by the *understanding*, not the intuitive faculty. *Understanding* is referred to under various descriptions in the Kant selection in §16.5 of *Lovers of Wisdom*; "the faculty of thinking", "the faculty of concepts", "the faculty of judgments", "the faculty of rules." Insofar as it is a faculty of concepts, the understanding supplies what is necessary to turn *perceiving* into *perceiving as* (we saw above, concepts are necessary for *perceiving as*.).[74]

---

[73]Another way to keep objects distinguished from things-in-themselves is to remember that objects exist in space and time. (Recall the discussion of this sentence in §16.4 of *Lovers of Wisdom*.) Space and time, however, are "forms of intuition", and not properties of things in themselves. So, objects are not things-in-themselves.

[74]There has been a great deal of debate concerning the issue of whether there is any such thing as pure perception with no conceptual component. Philosophers who believe that there is such pure perception refer to it as "the given" or "raw sense data." Philosophers who believe that there is no such pure perception often state their position by saying that all perception is "theory laden." In other words, these philosophers believe that whatever you perceive, you are always perceiving it *as* something or other.

But the understanding does not only supply the concepts that turn a perception of some object into a perception of the object as a such-and-such (that is, an object of some particular kind). The understanding also supplies concepts that are necessary *for the experience of any object whatsoever.*

These concepts -- the concepts that are a necessary condition of all experience -- comprise what Kant calls the 'categories of the understanding.' What is an example of such a category? One of the categories of the understanding is 'unity.' And since "what is not truly *one* being is not truly one *being*,"[75] each object, necessarily, is perceived as being *one* object. To this extent, the concept of unity is a concept that is necessary for the experience of any object as an object. And yet there is no object that is *identical* to unity. So, every object is a unity, but no object is unity itself. Each category of the understanding is like unity in this way: it can be predicated of every possible object of experience, but is not identical to any possible object of experience.

Reason, however, generates its "pure" concepts in an attempt to "complete" given concepts of the understanding. As a result, its concepts transcend all possible experience (hence they are "pure"). Consider the category of unity. As we said above, every object is a unity. For instance, the book you are reading is one object. But, this book is also a multiplicity in that it is made of many parts, e.g., many pages. So, your book, though a unity, is not *completely* unified. Reason thus constructs from the category of unity, the pure concept of complete unity (without multiplicity) -- "the substantial." This pure concept, like the category of unity, is not identical to any possible object of experience. But, unlike the category of unity, it cannot be predicated of any possible object of experience. While the predicate "is a unity" is true of *every* possible object of experience, the predicate "is a complete unity (predicable of nothing and without multiplicity)" is true of *no* possible object of experience.

Kant calls the substantial (complete unity) a "psychological idea." For, he claims, "the I" (the ego, the self, the soul) appears to be such a complete unity or "simple substance."[76] But, Kant, having read his Hume, knew of the problems with the view that we are aware of a self. And he agreed: the "I" (a simple, permanent, completely unified subject) is not a possible object of experience. Kant's "psychological idea," therefore, is an idea of a noumenal self.

Reason, with its pure concept of the substantial, attempts to complete the category of unity generated by the activity of the understanding. In doing so, however, unlike the understanding, it transcends all possible experience.[77]

Exercise
Classify the following as descriptions of

(a) an act of the faculty of intuition
(b) an act of the faculty of understanding
(c) an act of the faculty of reason

_____1. The creation of the blackness of the inkblots presently in your visual field.
_____2. Contemplation of the age and size of the universe.
_____3. Coming to know that all objects of experience are in time and space.

How Synthetic Apriori Knowledge is Possible
In sum, we have classified **judgments** into four different types: (i) analytic *apriori*, (ii) analytic *aposteriori*, (iii) synthetic *aposteriori*, (iv) synthetic *apriori*. **Synthetic *apriori*** judgments

---

[75]Remember this quote from Leibniz in Chapter 12 of *Lovers of Wisdom*?
[76]Kant shows his Leibnizian background in associating "simple substance" and "soul." Recall that Leibniz thought that every simple substance (or monad) is a soul which perceives the entire universe more or less clearly.
[77]There are two other pure concepts of reason which Kant discusses in his metaphysical works: the cosmological idea (which is the completion of the category of causality), and the theological idea (which is the completion of the category of possibility).

are peculiar in that they are **true** in virtue of the way the (phenomenal) world is, and yet are **known** independently of experience. Experience (and so every possible object of experience), is made possible by the **forms of intuition** and the **categories of the understanding**. Since the world of experience is *made possible* by these forms and categories, they are *necessary conditions* for the world of experience and all of its objects. **So**, the mind, in understanding the structure of its own faculties, can discover necessary conditions to which all possible objects of experience must conform, and thereby discover truths about all objects of experience, without appeal to the experience of any object in particular.

This is how synthetic *apriori* knowledge is possible.

Technical Correction

Technically, the statement that synthetic judgments are based on objects is not completely accurate. This is only true for a certain subclass of synthetic judgments. If in a synthetic judgment the predicate is not contained in the concept of the subject, then what exactly is the relation between the predicate and the concept of the subject which makes some particular synthetic judgment true? There are

Three classes of synthetic judgments:

      (i) judgments of experience,
      (ii) mathematical judgments, and
      (iii) metaphysical judgments.

(i) In the case of judgments of experience, the truth of the judgment is based on the object which is the subject of the judgment. These judgments are synthetic *aposteriori*. For example, your judgment that there is a book before you is a synthetic judgment of experience which you know *aposteriori*. It is made true by the (phenomenal) object before you. (ii) In the case of mathematical judgments, the connection between the predicate and the concept of the subject is based on *apriori* forms of intuition. (Space and time are the *apriori* forms of intuition. On Kant's view, geometrical judgments are based on the pure *apriori* intuition of space, while arithmetical judgments are based on the pure *apriori* intuition of time.) These judgments are synthetic *apriori*. (iii) In the case of metaphysical judgments the connection between the predicate and the concept of the subject is based on pure concepts of the understanding, and these judgments are synthetic *apriori*. We have limited the discussion in this chapter to the case of synthetic judgments of experience to make the distinction between analytic and synthetic judgments easier to draw. For greater detail see Kant's *Prolegomena*, especially §2 of the preamble; "Concerning the kind of cognition which can alone be called metaphysical".

Chapter 17

Hegel and the German Idealists

Absolute Rational Criticism

In previous chapters we discussed the process of rational criticism. We have characterized this as a developmental process of theory construction in which (i) the limitations of a given theory (T) are made explicit by revealing an inherent shortcoming of or providing a counterexample to T; and (ii) T is modified to overcome the limitations revealed in (i). Up to this point, rational criticism has been presented as a process in which *human beings* engage, most notably, perhaps, when they "philosophize." Hegel, however, did not see this process (which he called "dialectic") merely as something which people are involved in when they think philosophically.

According to Hegel, *reality itself* is involved in rational criticism. Reality is a Mind involved in rational criticism at all times. It is thought thinking itself toward its own actualization. Thus, the history of the world is seen by Hegel as the process of the development of one mind's awareness of itself. This mind he calls "the Absolute."

In order to understand how the Absolute mind is engaged in rational criticism, let's return to a general theme that has already appeared in one guise or another in previous chapters above and in *Lovers of Wisdom*. The theme, most generally put, is this: a *process* of transformation is initiated by an *opposition* necessitated by a *limitation* of some sort (usually an epistemological limitation due to the categories and finitude of reason). The process of transformation ends in (or eternally approaches) a state of *unification* of what previously was or appeared to be divided. For instance, recall the Pythagorean's discovery of irrational numbers (discussed above and in Chapter 1 of *Lovers of Wisdom*). Initially, the concepts of number and irrationality (in the mathematical sense -- that is, not being a ratio of integers) were *opposed*: The Pythagoreans believed that the only kinds of numbers are rational numbers. But it was discovered that this conception of number is *limited*: Irrational numbers were proven to exist. The philosophically minded Pythagoreans, remember, responded by *unifying* the concepts of number and irrationality.[78]

So we see in these examples, that through rational (cognitive) activity, a transformation is affected: concepts that are initially opposed to one another -- that seem to be incompatible with each other -- are united after the limitations of this opposition are made explicit. We can use this theme to understand how Hegel's Absolute is supposed to engage in rational criticism. For the Absolute develops its awareness of itself only by opposing itself to itself, in a sort of rational self-deception. That is, reason, with its contradictory categories, gives rise in the Absolute to the illusion of "otherness." And, in doing so, the Absolute becomes aware of itself *as such*. Hegel is saying that reality thinks, and that in thinking, reality fools itself into thinking that it is not everything. Reality divides itself, marks out its territory, establishes borders and boundaries. reality limits itself, in an act of rational self-deception. And it is through this act of self-deception that reality fully reveals itself to itself. But this takes time. This is what history is: *thought thinking itself toward its own actualization.*.

So Hegel's view is that reality opposes itself to itself, and in this act of opposition, reality limits itself and gives rise to 'otherness.' But over time, the sphere of 'otherness' diminishes: reality learns that it is everything, and that there is nothing other than it. Thus,

---

[78]Also recall, from Chapter 1 above, how Socrates learned how wisdom and ignorance are compatible, and, from Chapter 8 above, how Nicholas of Cusa argued that *all* opposites are *one* in the infinite.

the history of the world is nothing other than reality coming to realize that it is *everything*. The history of the world is nothing other than reality learning about itself through its past mistakes. This history of the world is nothing other than reality engaging in rational criticism with itself! Thus, not only the activity of philosophers and the philosophically minded, but *the very movement of time and all that takes place in it*, the movement away from the past and toward the future, through the present, is an activity of *thinking*.

Exercises:

1.   Hegel is called an "Absolute Idealist." Idealism is most generally characterized as the view that mind is the only reality, or that every thing that exists is a mental entity. You have encountered idealist views in connection with Berkeley (Chapter 14) and Kant (Chapter 16), as well as in connection with the other philosophers in Chapter 17 of *Lovers of Wisdom*. Briefly define the various forms of idealism in the spaces below, bringing out their similarities and their differences.

Berkelean Idealism (Berkeley):
Transcendental Idealism (Kant):
Subjective Idealism (Fichte):
Objective Idealism (Schelling):
Absolute Idealism (Hegel):

2.   By now you are well aquatinted with the activity of rational criticism. In Chapter 17 of *Lovers of Wisdom* you read about Hegel's "dialectic." Additionally, Kolak discusses stages of the development of thought as presented in Hegel's *The Encyclopedia of the Philosophical Sciences in Outline*. We take these to be three characterizations of the same developmental process, and each of the three characterizations of this process involves its own three stages or "moments." Below is a randomized list of the stages. Fill in the blanks below with the correct ordering and grouping of these names.

Anti-thesis
The idea in and for itself
Theory
The idea comes back to itself out of otherness
Thesis
Counterexample
Synthesis
The idea in its otherness
Revised theory

	Rational Criticism	**Dialectic**	**Stage of Thought Development**
(i)	_____	_____	_____
(ii)	_____	_____	_____
(iii)	_____	_____	_____

3. Define "sublation" and identify which stage of the above three-staged process corresponds to it.

4. Define "estrangement," or "alienation," (in Hegel's sense) and identify which stage of the above three-staged process corresponds to it.

93

Chapter 18

Kierkegaard and Nietzsche

Kierkegaard

We saw in the last chapter that Hegel gave a supreme status to rational criticism. His dialectic can be characterized as a "both/and" progression: it begins with a thesis, moves to an anti-thesis, and finally to a synthesis of *both* the thesis *and* the anti-thesis. Kierkegaard, on the other hand, balked at this, insisting that an existing, individual human being lives (whether he likes it or not) according to an "either/or" dialectic, a process of committing to decisions between competing alternatives. Rational criticism is replaced by *irrational commitment*.

At the heart of Kierkegaard's philosophy is the concept of "the absurd" (the word "absurd" from its Latin roots means "without sound"). The point here is that in facing the world as an existing human being, one is forced to choose between alternative actions, but, ultimately, is not given any reason whatsoever to pick one rather than the other of the alternatives. Recall the passage from *Either/Or* quoted in *Lovers of Wisdom*. Whichever alternative you choose, you will regret it. We must therefore commit without reason. It is this *act* of commitment without reason that invokes the passion by which alone an individual can transcend herself.

Since each alternative is as bad (or good) as the other, *what* you chose is irrelevant. What is important is *how* you choose, and whether you live up to that commitment. It is the *way* you do what you do, that ultimately makes it valuable. To do something in "just any old way" just will not do. Take a concrete example. Right now you are reading this book. "Why?," Kierkegaard says, is ultimately the wrong question. The fact is that you don't *have* to be reading this book now (or at any time). It is completely and entirely by your and only your choice that you are right now reading this book. "But," you may reply, "it is the assignment. I didn't make up the assignment. I have to do my homework or I will fail." This, of course is completely irrelevant. No one is *making* you do the assignment. You could right now just as well choose not to do the assignment, and perhaps fail your class. If there is right now someone physically pulling your eyelids open and holding your head so that you cannot even rotate your eyeballs in order to avoid the page, then that would be *pretty close* to being forced to read this. But, even there you have a choice. Why not just stare at the page blankly?

The important thing to realize is that, whatever you do, *you* choose to do it. But, you could choose to do the opposite for some other equally good reason. So, if *the way in which* you do what you do does not involve a passionate commitment (in spite of the recognition that your doing one thing rather than another is ultimately arbitrary), then, says Kierkegaard, you are not living the truth. Live the truth!

Chapter 19

The Social Philosophers

In Chapter 1, you learned that Protagoras used rational criticism to engender a shift in the predominant philosophical perspective of the time. His bucket experiment was meant to show that it makes little sense to theorize about a reality that transcends human experience. Protagoras instead argued that rational activity should be used in ways that improve humanity and the world. In nineteenth century Europe, a similar shift in philosophical perspective occurred. Rather than using rationality to improve *theories*, the social philosophers argued that we should use reason in order to change and improve the condition of *society*.

Compte, not unlike Epicurus, believed that humanity could fully realize its potentials only if everything was understood *scientifically*. In agreement with this idea, Mill furthered Compte's program by arguing that freedom of opinion was necessary for complete human development. Finally, Marx had the important insight that certain economic and material conditions are crucial to human realization. Thus, Compte, Mill and Marx each theorized about a different aspect of humanity that they regarded as necessary for full human development: Compte concentrated on the *intellectual* aspect of humanity; Mill concentrated on *ethical and political* aspects; and Marx concentrated on the *economic* aspect. Remembering Mill's important insight that several different theories can contain, "part of the truth; sometimes a greater, sometimes a smaller part...," it is reasonable to think that Compte, Mill and Marx each articulate part of the truth concerning the development of the human species. Let's review each of these important theories.

Compte

The Theological, the Metaphysical, and the Scientific

Intellectual development is a crucial element in Compte's picture of human development. He says,

> [E]ach of our leading conceptions -- each branch of our knowledge, -- passes successively through three different theoretical conditions: the Theological, or fictitious; The Metaphysical or abstract; and the Scientific, or positive.

Think of each "theoretical condition" as a *mode* of understanding phenomena. What characteristics distinguish the Theological, the Metaphysical, and the Scientific modes? Suppose that we want to understand why the snowflake has its symmetrical shape. If we reason that God is the cause of this shape, for example, then we are operating in the *Theological* mode. In this mode, phenomena are made intelligible by appealing to the wills, intentions, and activities of supernatural beings.[79] If, however, we reason that snowflakes are symmetrically shaped since they partake in some Platonic form, then we are operating in the *Metaphysical* mode. For when operating in the Metaphysical mode, phenomena are understood not by appealing to the wills or intentions of beings, but instead to abstract entities. Finally,

---

[79]If you recall Chapter 4, the common belief that gods and goddesses caused events on earth (against which Epicurus' was arguing), is also an example of operating in the Theological mode.

if, on the basis of observation and repeated experiment, we reason that the atomic structure of water, temperature, and various meteorological conditions explain why the snowflake is shaped as it is, then we are operating in the *Scientific* mode. In this mode, phenomena are made intelligible by appealing to laws that are formulated in accord with reason, experiment, and observation.[80]

According to Compte, each of the three modes corresponds to a stage in the *evolution* of human understanding. The understanding is in its infancy in the Theological mode. And after passing through the Metaphysical stage, it reaches full maturity in the *Scientific* mode:

Examples of the Three Modes of the Evolution of Human Understanding

Evolution of human Understanding	**Scientific** mode: The *atomic structure* of the snowflake and the *conditions of the environment* explain why the snowflake is symmetrically shaped.
	Metaphysical mode: The snowflake is symmetrically shaped because it partakes in the "form of symmetry."
	Theological mode: The will of *God* explains why the snowflake is symmetrically shaped.

In the above figure, we can see that the idea that something "explains" the shape of the snowflake appears in all three modes. That is, in each of the three modes it is supposed that there is some *reason why* the snowflake is symmetrically shaped. It seems natural for us to feel that there is some reason why the snowflake exhibits a symmetrical structure (whatever we take that reason to be).

But why is this? *Why* is it so natural to assume that things happen for a reason? Compte's view suggests an answer along the following lines: we are aware (in some sense) of our own action as being purposeful. We perform many of our actions for *reasons*, and these actions cause changes in our environment. Then, in the initial mode (the Theological mode) of understanding both ourselves and the world, we attribute a similar purposefulness to the causes of natural events. We personify the world. And even after literal personifications of natural events, such as gods of the sea and goddesses of the changing of seasons, have withered away, and we have "ascended" to the next mode, there is still this sense that things happen for a reason. And so Compte claims that, "there is no science which, having attained the positive stage, does not bear marks of having passed through the others." Just as an adult maintains some of the characteristics of its youth, the fully developed understanding has the germ of its "naiveté" (its theological and metaphysical characteristics) still buried within it.

Rational Criticism and Compte's Theoretical Modes

In our earlier chapters, we have seen that rational criticism promotes the advancement of the understanding. Recall how the philosophically minded Pythagoreans reacted to the discovery of irrational magnitudes. Originally thinking that only rational numbers existed, the Pythagoreans furthered their understanding of the concept of "number" by changing their theory to include *irrational* numbers. The *advancement* of the understanding promoted by

---

[80] *All* phenomena, according to Compte, are law governed, even *social* phenomena. Note that Compte believes he has discovered one of the laws of human development with his doctrine of the three stages of intellectual development:

> From the study of the development of human intelligence, in all
> directions, and through all times, the discovery arises of a great
> fundamental law...The law is this: -- that each of our leading
> conceptions, -- each branch of our knowledge, -- passes successively
> through three different theoretical conditions.

rational criticism is indeed similar to the *evolution* of the understanding as described by Compte. Note how the Pythagorean's new theory includes an aspect of their original one:

The Old World Implicit in the New

Advancement of Understanding	New theory : Rational and irrational numbers exist.
	Original theory: Rational numbers exist.

Although Compte's notion of the evolution of the understanding bears a resemblance to the advancement of the understanding that rational criticism produces, there are several differences. First, note that although the understanding of the Pythagoreans' is advanced through rational criticism, it fails to evolve through all three Comtean modes. Assuming that numbers are abstract entities, we can say that the understanding of the Pythagoreans operates solely in the *Metaphysical* mode. Thus, one can engage in rational criticism without moving from one mode to another. Presumably, on Compte's view, if one engaged in rational criticism for a long enough time, one would move out of one mode and into the next.

Second, note that the understanding, when it is fully ripened in the Scientific mode, involves *observation*. The philosophers whom we have seen engaging in rational criticism, however, typically did not do so in a way which involved observation. The Milesians, Pythagoreans, and Plato, to name a few, all believed that the eyes were not windows, and accordingly made no appeal to observation in their descriptions of reality. According to Compte, however, any mode of understanding which ignores observation is not fully matured.

Why does Compte believe that operating in the Scientific mode is a precondition of full human development? Note that operating in both the Theological and Metaphysical modes leads to *disagreement*. Not only are there different theological accounts regarding the creation of the Universe,[81] but there are also different metaphysical accounts regarding the nature of reality.[82] According to Compte, unlike the Theological and Metaphysical modes, the Scientific mode commands *agreement* since it involves reason *and observation*. Indeed, when theorizing about a reality that we are all observing, the possibility of disagreement is significantly reduced.[83] By operating in a mode of understanding that commands agreement, claims Compte, society flourishes, and humanity progresses.

Mill

The Individual and Society

Mill, who was as concerned with the good of humanity as Compte, narrowed his philosophical scope and focused on the good of the *individual*. According to Mill, an individual can only be fully developed, can only actualize her potentials, if she lives in a society which not only permits *individual freedom* (only restricting it when it harms others), but also respects the *happiness of the majority*.

---

[81] For example, Avicenna and Al-Farabi (both Islamic theologians) believed that the Universe is eternal. According to Christian theologians, however, God *created* the universe.

[82] For instance, Plato believed that Reality consisted in forms, and Anaximander believed that Reality consisted in "the infinite boundless."

[83] Operating in the Scientific mode surely does not command *universal* agreement, as there are many debates among scientists. For instance, evolutionary biologists are divided on the issue of whether altruistic behavior is an *individual* or a *group* selected trait. Furthermore, as you learned in Chapter 9, astronomers were divided on the issue of whether our solar system is a geocentric or a heliocentric one. Even though there may not be universal agreement in the Scientific mode, scientists can at least agree on *methods of inquiry*. The underdetermination of a theory by empirical evidence that you read about in Chapter 9 above, indeed contributes to disagreement in the Scientific mode. But the issue of whether the principle of the underdetermination of theories is a legitimate principle, does not enjoy universal agreement among scientists and philosophers of science!

Let's consider this claim. Advocating that a certain kind of social order is necessary for self-development, Mill is arguing that self-development requires circumstances that are *external* to the individual. For, Mill believes that self-development can only occur within a society which, in addition to granting its members the liberty to pursue their own course of life, also respects the happiness of the majority of its members. Thus, Mill, like Marx (as we will soon discuss) thinks that self-development is *context dependent*.[84]

But in exactly what way, you should be asking yourself, is the individual's development dependent on her society? Well, an important consequence of individual liberty that is extensively discussed by Mill, is the ability to *think* and to *believe* freely. And what is bound to happen within a society whose members are permitted to think and believe freely? The citizens of this society are sure to *disagree*. And when someone disagrees with you, you are forced to reflect and reexamine your own beliefs (about the world and about yourself). In fact, Mill thinks that disagreement brings us nearer to the truth:

> It still remains to speak of the principal causes which make diversity of opinion advantageous, and will continue to do so until mankind shall have entered a stage of intellectual advancement which at present seems an incalculable distance...[1] the received opinion may be false, and some other opinion consequently true...or [2] the received opinion being true, a conflict with the opposite error is essential to a clear apprehension and deep feeling of its truth...[or] [3] when the conflicting doctrines ...share the truth between them; and the non conforming opinion is needed to supply the remainder of the truth...

In this important passage, Mill describes three beneficial kinds of disagreement.[85] In the first case, the accepted opinion (or theory) is completely wrong, and some another completely right. In the second case, the accepted opinion is right and some other wrong, but the correctness of the former opinion can only be clearly and fully perceived if it clashes against the latter. In the third type of disagreement, the two conflicting opinions are *partly* true, but each opinion needs the other in order to evolve into a fully true opinion.

Disagreement is valuable because, in at least three different ways, it brings one closer to the truth. So, an individuals development is dependent upon a society that permits individual liberty, and thereby, disagreement. For by living in such a society, a citizen is more likely to apprehend the truth, and to help others apprehend the truth. Disagreement and

---

[84] One might object, after reading Locke, that individual liberty does not depend on a certain type of social organization. For Locke says in his *Second Treatise of Government* that men are free *by nature* (see Chapter 13):

> MEN BEING, AS HAS BEEN SAID, *by nature* all free, equal, and independent, no one can be put out of his estate and subjected to the political power of another without his own consent ... (our emphasis).

One only has to look at modern examples of slavery to know that, in all practicality, the political organization of a country determines which rights are given to its members. The thousands of workers from countries like the Philippines and Bangladesh, who migrate to other countries like Japan and South Korea in order to work low paying jobs, while denied virtually all significant rights, for instance, is nothing less than a modern form a slavery. The case of Iqbal Misah, moreover, a 12 year old youth labor activist, who, after freeing himself from 8 years of slavery at a Pakistani rug factory, spoke out against youth labor, freed thousands of children, and awakened the modern world to the horrors of "bonded labor," provides a tragic example of modern slavery. After winning the 1995 Reebok award for humane services, 12 year old Iqbal was murdered on Easter Sunday, while riding on his bicycle with his friends. The Pakistani "rug Mafia" was blamed. These cases, among others, support the idea that freedom is granted and respected by political bodies, and is not "innate."

[85] cf. Aristotle's taxonomy of opposites in Chapter 10 of his *Categories*: "Things are said to be opposed in four senses: (i) as correlatives to one another, (ii) as contraries to one another, (iii) as privatives to positives, (iv) as affirmatives to negatives." (The translation is Richard McKeon's in *The Basic Works of Aristotle*, Random House, 1941.) Respective examples of these types of oppositions are (i) "double" and "half," (ii) "bad" and "good," (iii) "blindness" and "sight," and (iv) "He sits" and "He does not sit."

debate increase both the chances of comprehending the truth, on the one hand, and the probabilities of both individual and social realization, on the other.

Rational Criticism as a Species of Disagreement

In thinking that disagreement is beneficial, is Mill thinking of the kind of disagreement involved in *rational criticism?* We mentioned in the earlier chapters that, in the first stage of rational criticism, one *criticizes* a theory. In the first stage of rational criticism, in other words, one shows *why* one disagrees with a theory by offering a criticism, thereby making one's reasons for disagreement explicit. We well know by now, that this activity can be beneficial, but does Mill think that the disagreement involved in rational criticism is beneficial?

In order to answer this question, let us return to the philosophically minded Pythagoreans' use of rational criticism. Their original theory that "only rational numbers exist," if you recall, conflicted with the proof of irrational magnitudes. In reacting to this proof, the philosophically minded Pythagoreans changed their view to include irrational numbers, and therefore engaged in rational criticism. Let us call their original theory "opinion (i)," and the conflicting proof "opinion (ii)." Thus:

Opinion (i) = Only rational numbers exist.
Opinion (ii) = The existence of irrational magnitudes can be proved.

Exercise
1. Look at the above and determine whether the philosophically minded Pythagoreans took these two opinions to exemplify any of the types of disagreement described by Mill. In other words, do you think that opinion (i) and opinion (ii) conflict in a manner such that

[1] One opinion is completely right, and the other is completely wrong *and/or*
[2] one opinion is right and the other wrong, but the correctness of one of these opinions can only be clearly perceived if it clashes against the other *and/or*
[3] Both opinions are partly true, but each opinion needs the other in order to be *completely* true ?

Explain your answer in writing before you move on.

The most obvious kind of conflict that opinion 1 and opinion 2 exhibit is the third kind. The original theory of the philosophically minded Pythagoreans was *partly* right since rational numbers *do* exist. Similarly, it is true that irrational numbers exist, but irrational numbers are not the *only* kinds of numbers that exist. Thus, Mill's taxonomy of disagreement subsumes the kind of disagreement often involved in rational criticism. Indeed, Mill would presumably say that the Pythagoreans benefited by being exposed to a divergent opinion about the nature of number.

Marx

We mentioned above that, like Mill, Marx thinks of self-development as context dependent. But while Mill focuses on ethical and political preconditions of self-development, Marx focuses on the *economic* preconditions. According to Marx, the economic base of a society significantly shapes the behavior and consciousness of its members. If we think that survival is a 'human instinct,' then it is easy to see why Marx makes this claim. For the economic base of society dictates how individuals are to survive within the society. How are you going to make a living? The society in which you live *determines* the options from which you can choose.

Marx insists that self-development *cannot* occur within a society in which capitalism is the economic base. Why does he say this? Within a capitalist society, economic activity is fueled by competition among the "owners of the means of production" (referred to by Marx as the "bourgeoisie"), or, in other words, big businesses, of which there are only few. Because prices are so competitive, in order for these owners to make a profit, workers (referred to by Marx as the "proletariat"), of which there are many, are paid only what their basic survival requires. And workers, since they have to survive, *will* work for these wages. And so, he says, such labor is not voluntary, but *forced*.

If you have ever had a job that you disliked, but nonetheless remained as a worker because you needed the money, you are familiar with what Marx is talking about. Imagine a worst-case scenario. Initially, perhaps, you don't mind the job because it is "new;" new faces to see, new facts to learn. Eventually, you become familiar with this new environment, and then comfortable, and then bored, and then completely unaware that you are dedicating your life to an activity for which you have no love at all. Just because you do not, in some single act of self-conscious assertion, *dedicate* yourself to, say, your job, this does not mean that you don't dedicate your life to it. If you spend forty, fifty hours a week at your job, spend your nights before the TV for a few hours before drifting asleep, attend an occasional party, and take a once a year trip, you have dedicated your life to your job. Or better, your life has been dedicated to your job because you never dedicated it to anything else, to anything you really loved. And as time goes by you are gradually taken from yourself, and then that's it. "He who cannot obey himself," wrote Nietzsche, "is commanded." We hope the relevance is clear.

Alienation

The scenario we have been describing is a version of what Marx calls "alienation." This concept is the key to understanding why Marx believes that self-development is impossible within a capitalist society. Since the members of the working class are forced to work for menial wages, the worker is reduced to a mere tool, a commodity of the bourgeois. The worker, in other words, becomes alienated from the very things that enable him to survive, flourish and develop.

Think about activities that you do *not* find alienating, that you (in contrast) *love* to do, and ask yourself what happens to you when you do them. What is gained? Well, that thing that is gained, without such activities, cannot be had. And that thing is required for self-development. In this way, alienating labor prevent self-development?

Marx suggests that what makes self-development a *possibility*, is the *union* of an individual with his activity and product. For by engaging in these sorts of activities, both the understanding of ourselves and the world is deepened, and as our understanding deepens, our experience becomes more rich. In a society with *communism* as its economic base, claims Marx, it is possible to survive by engaging in these sorts of activities. In arguing that a communist economy is a precondition for human development, Marx implies that self-development requires *individual freedom*. For in order to determine which activities with which we can unite, we must be able to explore a *multitude* of activities -- our labor must not be forced, but *voluntary*.

In offering his economic theory of communism as a theory in which the alienation of the worker is eliminated, Marx engages in rational criticism against the theory of capitalism. After criticizing capitalism since it necessitates alienation, and hence prevents the actualization of its members, Marx accordingly offers communism as a theory that he believes is immune to this criticism. It is interesting to note that, the United States operates by a capitalist economy, and is known for granting its members individual freedom. Do you think that the United States grants the kind of freedom which Marx takes to be necessary for self-development? Do you think that in the United States, labor is not forced, but voluntary? Think about these two questions, and make your answers explicit to yourself. If you are lucky, you will find someone who disagrees with you.

Exercises

2.   Do you think that the United States grants the kind of freedom which Marx takes to be necessary for self-development?

3.   Do you think that in the United States, labor is not forced, but voluntary?

Chapter 20

The American Experience

Pragmatism

The American philosophers of Chapter 20 in *Lovers of Wisdom* emphasize a new way of understanding the notions of truth and reality. Their philosophical movement has come to be called *pragmatism*. The movement is fairly complicated since it not only addresses many standard philosophical issues, but is also a philosophy about philosophy. Let us here attempt to put American pragmatism into perspective.

The history of intellectual thought may be seen as a series of framework shifts -- that is, as a series of changes in perspective or conceptual organization. Each shift is motivated by the limitations of the previous framework. Indeed, every (finite) framework is limited in that it does not have the resources to solve every problem. When an old framework is exhausted of its resources to solve a set of problems, then it is time to evolve philosophically -- it is time to develop a new perspective on the problem at hand. This is just the method of rational criticism, discussed at length in previous chapters. Examples permeate the entire history of philosophy, and so, can be found throughout *Lovers of Wisdom* and the companion presently in your hands: Aristotle's theory of substance replaced Plato's theory of forms, Locke's theory of knowledge replaced Descartes', Hume's empiricism replaced Locke's, and so on. The fruitfulness of a change in philosophical perspective is marked by both its utility in getting us closer to solutions to old problems, and by its ability to clarify the problems themselves.

Pragmatism represents a major shift in philosophical perspective. Pragmatists see all of philosophy from Descartes to Kant (modern philosophy) as an exhausted way of understanding things -- exhausted, because it ultimately fails to solve 2000 year-old philosophical problems. As we will see below, pragmatists challenge the theory of truth that has been assumed by traditional philosophy. It is their conception of truth, claim the Pragmatist, that renders the traditional philosophical problems insoluble. Accordingly, the pragmatists offer a new conception of truth, and therewith, a new conception of reality and our place within it.

The Correspondence Theory of Truth

Prior to the pragmatists, a certain notion of truth dominated philosophy; the *correspondence theory of truth*. It is this theory of truth that the pragmatists challenge. The correspondence theory defines truth as a *relation* between beliefs or sentences, on the one hand, and the mind and language-independent world, on the other. In other words, truth is correspondence between our mental world, and the Real, objective world. Essentially, the correspondence theory says that we have true belief when our understanding of the world, mirrors the way that the world really is. A sentence or belief is true when it corresponds to objective reality. And when a sentence (or belief) corresponds to reality, there is some feature of reality that renders the sentence true.

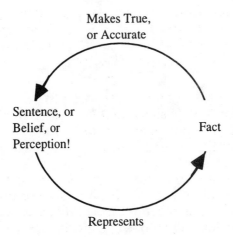

Makes True,
or Accurate

Sentence, or
Belief, or
Perception!

Fact

Represents

For example, the sentence 'John won the race' is true, if and only if John did win. If John did not cross the finish line first, then the sentence is false.[86] In order for a sentence to be true, it must represent some feature of the world -- some fact.

The pragmatists believe that the correspondence theory precludes the solubility of many philosophical problems. Why? Well, the correspondence theory of truth is traditionally *dualistic* in that it attempts to characterize a relation between two radically distinct kinds of stuff -- either mental stuff (perceptions and beliefs) and the mind-independent world (facts, states of affairs, etc.) or linguistic stuff (beliefs and sentences) and the language-independent world (facts, states of affairs, etc.). According to the pragmatists, once we accept the correspondence theory, with its dualistic picture of truth, we are faced with the age-old problem of skepticism.

The Correspondence Theory of Truth and Skepticism

The problem of skepticism is the problem that all our beliefs might be false. One must escape this problem by somehow showing that this possibility is not an actuality. But how, with a correspondence theory of truth, can one escape this problem? How can such a theorist prove that all of our beliefs (and perceptions) are not false? The correspondence theory puts us on one side of a veil of perceptions and theories. Reality, on this view, falls on the other side. Truth involves a relation between *both* sides of the veil, but we have access to only *one* side. We are, as it were, "trapped" inside our perceptions, our languages and our theories -- and nothing could be understood without these entrapments. But if we only have access to our perceptions, languages and theories -- if we only have access to stuff on this side of the veil -- how could we ever tell whether these things 'match up' with reality (things on the other side)? How could we establish that our picture of the world mirrors the world? And if we cannot determine whether our perceptions and theories mirror reality, then how can we know that they are true? We can't!

This is an example of how the correspondence theory of truth precludes the solubility of philosophical problems. The skeptic argues that any purported solution to these problems might be false, and if we hold the correspondence theory of truth, we cannot prove her wrong. Since we are unable to show that our perceptions and theories, do in fact, mirror reality, we are unable to respond to the skeptic. Even worse, the correspondence theory forces us to admit that *correspondence, and hence truth, cannot be humanly detected.* (It is perhaps hard to believe that our common sense view of truth, seems to imply that we cannot prove that anything is true.)

Advocates of the correspondence theory of truth have attempted to solve the problem of skepticism by specifying an intermediary between the knower and known -- an epistemically privileged go-between that is supposed to secure (for the most part) our knowledge of reality. For Plato it was the forms, and, for Descartes, it was clear and distinct

---

[86]Unless, of course, the person who crossed the finish line first was disqualified, etc. But, you get the drift.

ideas (such as "I think; therefore I am"). For Locke it was just the fact that we have ideas that are best explained as being caused by reality. Such causal intermediaries between knowers and reality are intended to guarantee that (at least some or most of) our beliefs are true. They function to preclude the possibility of us being completely wrong about everything.

The Pragmatist Response

According to the pragmatist, the positing of epistemically privileged intermediaries between us and the world only augments the unknowability of the real world. For insofar as these intermediaries justify beliefs at all, they must be interpreted as having some feature(s) in virtue of which they guarantee our connection to reality. They must have some feature, more specifically, that makes our beliefs true -- that makes our apparent knowledge real knowledge. So these intermediaries must adequately justify our beliefs. According to the pragmatist, the only thing that can justify a belief is another belief. But such justifying beliefs cannot themselves be justified by further beliefs. Otherwise, they do not serve to *guarantee* truth.[87] But now, what is it about these intermediary beliefs that serves to guarantee truth? What feature do they possess, in virtue of which our knowledge is so secure? At this point one must theorize: it is in virtue of x that our intermediary beliefs tie our beliefs to the objective world. But to theorize is to do just that -- it is to theorize. And theories require further justifications for their adequacy. They require us to call us further beliefs in order to defend the theory. But then it seems that the epistemically privileged intermediaries are no longer privileged -- they now require justifications further than themselves. So no matter how hard we try to justify our beliefs by positing epistemically privileged intermediaries, we get no further than our own beliefs and theories. And so, contrary to the hope of the correspondence theorist, we don't really break on through to the other side of the veil of perception.

How can we know that the essences of things are adequately expressed by grasping Plato's forms? How can we know whether clear and distinct ideas are not, sometimes, wrong? How can we know that the ideas produced by mental habits have any connection to the world? We can only so know, if we have some theory about what the relevant features of such intermediaries are. But then we're back inside the world of appearances, we haven't connected our minds up to the mind-independent world.

Pragmatism can be seen, minimally, as the denial that truth is a relation of correspondence between mental (or linguistic) entities (beliefs, ideas, perceptions, thoughts, theories, etc.) and a mind-independent reality. And by denying the correspondence theory of truth, according to the pragmatist, epistemological skepticism looses its punch. But different pragmatists put different emphases on this claim. Some are willing to accept a watered-down version of the correspondence theory, while denying the sharp distinction between mind and world. Others allow the sharp dualism, but deny that correspondence constitutes truth. *Pragmatism*, then, may be defined as a theory of truth that either:

(i) reinterprets truth as correspondence between our theories and the *theory-laden* world (the watered down version of correspondence),

or

(ii) reinterprets truth solely as a property of *beliefs* about the world (rather than as a relation between beliefs and the world).

Strategy (i) redescribes truth as a correspondence between two things made of the same kind of stuff, and strategy (ii) allows for the radical differences in kind between mind and world while redescribing truth as a property of belief-systems only. Reality, then, is whatever such true beliefs are about. By the lights of this version of pragmatism, truth (and the way the world is independently of what we believe) is explained, in large part, by what we are

---

[87]Recall Descartes seach for absolute certainty in the *Meditations* (see Chapter 10). No belief is absolutely certain if there is any distance between it and the evidence for its truth, or between it and its truth-maker. Only a belief that gaurantees its own truth can bring with it absolute certaintly.

justified in believing -- whereas, on the correspondence theory, what we correctly believe is explained, in part, by what the truth is (independently of what we believe).

When the pragmatist takes truth to be a property of belief systems (rather than a relationship between beliefs and the world), she is sometimes called an idealist. But that is not necessarily to imply that she believes that the truth is nothing other than what we happen to arbitrarily believe. The pragmatist is not saying that truth is relative or subjective. That would be to deny the objectivity of truth, the objectivity of the way the world is. And if neither truth nor reality is objective, then there is no possibility of error. Yet, even a pragmatist wants to leave room for the possibility of having false beliefs. In fact, she probably wants to leave open the possibility of *everyone* being wrong about some things. What the pragmatist wants to say is that the truth is whatever we would determine to be the case given the best possible methods that we could employ *in principle*, under the best possible conditions. The Earth is round, if that is what would be determined by investigators with the best possible methods of investigating. (Note that this does not mean *our best present methods*, but the best possible methods given unlimited resources and technological development.) In this sense, all truth is knowable, according to this type of idealist. But that is not to say that all truth is known, or could be known in our lifetime. Truth, for the pragmatist, is ideal knowledge. That is why some of the pragmatists (for example, James and Royce) were called idealists.

Pragmatic strategies attempt to give reality back to the knower by dissolving a traditional boundary that severs the knower from reality. They appear to refute the skeptic and the possibility of global error (the possibility that all our beliefs are false). A traditional problem is dissolved!

Idealism: Berkeley and Peirce

Bishop Berkeley (see Chapter 14) was a perceptual idealist. He claimed that "to be is to be perceived." But he also said,

> The table I write on I say exists, that is, I see and feel it; and if I were out of my study I should say it existed -- meaning thereby that if I was in my study I might perceive it...[88]

In other words, to be is to be perceiv*able*. If nobody looks, the table does not cease to exist. Rather, the table exists, since one would see it in ideal circumstances. The crucial point is that idealism does not imply relativism or subjectivism, but rather constrains truth (and so reality) by *possible* knowledge.

What is the stuff of which X's are made? Berkeley claimed that nothing can be the object of a perception but another perception. He argued that for any imagined object X, X is itself an idea in someone's mind. So for any choice of X, X is a mental entity (an idea). Similarly, but more generally, C. S. Peirce argued that nothing can be represented that is not itself a representation. On Peirce's view, the whole of reality consists of signs. Signs are the stuff of which things (of any kind) are made. This thesis ignites Peirce's pragmatism. Signs are pieces of language. They are syntactic elements. If everything is composed of signs, then everything is fused with language. On this view, the world is essentially linguistic.

What are the consequences of Peirce's thesis? An obvious consequence is that a sharp distinction between language and world is dissolved. Without this distinction, the traditional correspondence theory no longer holds sway, since such a theory of truth constitutively involves a strict language-world dichotomy. The traditional view involves a notion of "world" free of linguistic constraints. As we noted, it this strong dichotomy that gives rise to the skeptical thesis that we might all be brains in vats (or more generally, that all our beliefs might be false), since it precludes the possibility of checking our beliefs against reality.

After the dissolution of correspondence, and with it the skeptical worry, Peirce sets out to characterize his own positive theory of truth. Since reality itself is a linguistic affair,

---

[88]Berkeley's *Treatise Concerning the Principles of Human knowledge*, section 3, found in *Lovers of Wisdom*, chapter 14, section 3.

truth should not be expected to outrun possible ways of understanding the world. Truth is intimately connected to our theories and language. Truth, according to Peirce, is what we would take to be true in ideal circumstance at the end of all our theorizing. If this is right, then all truth is knowable; no truth outruns our abilities to know it.

Notice that Peirce has turned the order of explanation on its head.

TRADITIONAL PICTURE

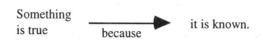

PEIRCE'S PICTURE

Traditionally, truth partially explained knowledge. It was mind- and language-independent aspects of the world that made some of our beliefs and theories about the world correct. Peirce seems to be saying that "knowledge" explains truth. That is, he seems to claim that our beliefs and theories somehow give rise to truth.

Pragmatism and Knowledge

Pragmatists characterize truth in terms of 'knowledge:' truth is what we are justified in believing. But knowledge is typically defined as justified, true, belief. So, how can pragmatists define truth without circularity? If the notion of 'knowledge' is supposed to help us understand the notion of truth, but the notion of knowledge presupposes an understanding of truth, then an explanation of truth in terms of knowledge will be uninformative. We will have learned nothing new from the explanation. To avoid the circularity of explanation, the pragmatists must also part with the traditional notion of knowledge. They must define knowledge not as justified, true belief, but as some sort of justified (or correct) belief.

Thus, in order to provide a non-circular definition of truth, pragmatists must explain what they mean by 'correct belief.' For Peirce, such a belief is one that is acquired scientifically. Thus all and only knowledge is scientific knowledge.[89] Scientific beliefs comprise knowledge, since science is a respectable, practical and successful enterprise. Importantly respectability, practicality and success are *pragmatic* considerations. And these pragmatic considerations -- the practical results of science --according to Peirce, legitimate science as a vehicle of knowledge, and hence, truth. For Peirce and for other pragmatists, pragmatic considerations determine knowledge, and knowledge determines truth.

Concluding

We have seen how the pragmatists offer a new perspective that dissolves the age old problem of skepticism. By denying the traditional correspondence theory of truth, pragmatists make knowledge possible. The pragmatists, by giving reality back to the knower, solve the problem of skepticism. This is indeed another instance of rational criticism: traditional

---

[89] For other pragmatists the notion of "correct belief" is left more open-ended, to include, but not to be exhausted by, scientific inquiry. History, culture and environment, as Dewey thought, must all be taken into consideration when trying to evaluate the correctness of belief.

philosophy, insofar as it assumed the correspondence theory of truth, was unable to show that knowledge of reality was even possible. The pragmatists made this problem explicit, and provided a theory of truth that made knowledge possible. What is the new picture of reality that the pragmatist provides? It surely is not like Kant's view that there is reality of things-in-themselves. For the pragmatist, the nature of reality is determined by pragmatic considerations. For the pragmatist, reality is what our best theories are about.

Exercise

For each of the remaining pragmatists (Dewey, James and Royce), determine which version of pragmatism is adopted: (i) a sharp mind-world dualism is rejected, or (ii) truth is reinterpreted solely as a property of *beliefs* about the world (rather than as a relation between beliefs and the world). Explain your answers.

Dewey:

James:

Royce:

Chapter 21

The European Experience

In several important ways, the philosophical movement initiated by Husserl, and further developed by Heidegger and Sartre, resembles the philosophical movement initiated by the Social philosophers, especially Compte, whom you read about in Chapter 19. Both the Social and the European philosophers, for instance, reacted against the traditional philosophical concern with the nature of an 'appearance transcendent reality.' The Social philosophers, recall, concerned themselves with the *development of humanity*, rather than with the nature of reality. In like manner, rather than occupying themselves with the traditional philosophical concern, the European philosophers concentrated on the *nature of human consciousness* and *human experience*. Both the Social and the European philosophers, therefore, were advocates of unique philosophical programs that put primary emphasis on human reality, rather than on a reality that transcended human experience.[90]

Husserl

The Method of Phenomenological Reduction

Husserl, like Compte, was concerned with the evolution -- the advancement -- of human understanding. Whereas Compte argued that human understanding evolves from the Theological to the Scientific mode, Husserl believed that the understanding could evolve from a *natural* attitude, to a *philosophical* one. According to Husserl, the method for achieving this evolution is the method of *phenomenological reduction*. Although rational criticism, as you have seen, is also a method by which the understanding can be moved into an enlightened state, phenomenological reduction differs in important ways from this method.

One of the ways in which phenomenological reduction and rational criticism differ, concerns the respective *dynamics* that characterize these types of evolution. Rational criticism, as you well know by now, is a two-step process in which (i) the problems of a theory are made explicit, and (ii) that theory is replaced with one that is less problematic. When phenomenological reduction is used to advance the understanding, however, very different steps are involved. After focusing on a specific experience, one then 'brackets' or *excises* from this experience the presuppositions and assumptions behind it. One strips the theory from the experience.

These two methods also differ insofar as they have different domains of application. We have described rational criticism as a method that sharpens and enriches *theories* (e.g., about the constituents of ultimate reality) and *concepts* (e.g., 'piety,' 'number,' etc.). Phenomenological reduction, on the other hand, is a process that directly affects *experience*. Further, phenomenological reduction has a domain of application that includes: (i) objects and images (e.g., a piece of chalk), (ii) the conception of time, and (iii) intellectual processes.

---

[90]We do not mean to suggest that the Social and the European philosophers were the *first* philosophers to focus on human experience. Protagoras, as well as the Hellenistic and Roman philosophers (Chapters 1 and 4, respectively) focused primarily on human experience, rather than the nature of an appearance transcendent Reality (indeed, Protagoras thought it fruitless to do so.)

Method	Steps in advancing the understanding	Domains of application of methods
Rational Criticism	(i). Show that a theory is problematic. (ii). Replace that theory with one which is less problematic.	(i) Theories (ii) Concepts
Phenomenological Reduction	(i) Focus on specific experience. (ii) Strip away, 'bracket' from this experience, all theoretical assumptions and presuppositions.	(i) Objects (ii) Conception of time (iii) Intellectual processes (e.g. calculating)

Below we will perform phenomenological reductions of type (i) (on an object) and type (iii) on an intellectual process.

The Phenomenological Reduction of an Object

To illustrate the method of phenomenological reduction, let's focus on our experience of the following figure:[91]

Recall the distinction between 'seeing' and 'seeing as.'[92] Like the duck/rabbit figure that you looked at earlier, this figure can be *seen as* two different things. On the one hand, you may perceive the above as an image of an ugly old hag (in left profile). On the other hand, however, you may perceive the above figure as an image of a young woman (facing away). The fact that you can see the figure in these two ways shows that your experiences are infused with certain assumptions and presuppositions.[93] Now, in the second step of

---

[91]This figure can be found in "Observation" by Norwood R. Hanson in *Theories and Observation in Science*, Richard E. Grandy (ed.), Prentice-Hall, 1973. It was created by the psychologist Edwin G. Boring.

[92]This distinction was discussed in Chapter 5 above in connection with Augustine's view of the mind's knowledge of itself, and, briefly, in Chapter 13 above in connection with "knowledge of kind."

[93]Expectations, assumptions, and presuppositions are constantly permeating experiences. When you experience this book for instance, you expect it to behave in a certain way, to function as a supplement to *Lovers of Wisdom*. If you were to turn the page and find the rest of the book blank, you would undoubtedly be surprised. One

phenomenological reduction, these assumptions are 'bracketed' and 'set aside.' In other words, in the second step of phenomenological reduction, one must bracket the fact that the above image can be perceived as either an old hag or as a young girl.

According to Husserl, experiences can be apprehended in their most 'pure' state if one brackets the assumptions and presuppositions that contribute to them. Indeed, Husserl believed that if we encountered objects and images without the usual assumptions, their *essences* would be apprehended. What is the essence of the above figure? Kolak mentions that phenomenological reduction is extremely formal and technical, and so if we were to be rigorous, we would express the essence of the above figure with mathematics and logic. But to simplify our task, let's use a familiar metaphor that illustrates the point. If you imagine a computer program that generates the above image, you will start to see what Husserl takes 'essences' to consist in. For such a program is apprehended neither as an ugly old hag, nor as a young girl. Rather, such a program is apprehended as a *structure* --as a piece of information consisting in interrelated parts. Recall Kolak's remark:

> Husserl focuses on a purely descriptive and non-theoretical account of consciousness to try and see directly how the world appears -- how the world "reveals itself" to consciousness...The purpose is to get "behind" the content of consciousness, where the deep structure of the world can reveal itself through the structure of consciousness.

This remark helps us to see what the fruit of phenomenological reduction -- the 'philosophical attitude' -- consists in. For, phenomenological reduction does not advance the understanding by spawning better theories about things. Nor does phenomenological reduction advance the understanding by enriching our concepts and language (as rational criticism does). Rather, phenomenological reduction advances the understanding by disclosing the structure through which the world is apprehended. Thus, the philosophical attitude consists in a cognizance of this structure -- in an awareness of that which remains unblemished by our theoretical assumptions and presuppositions. Simply put, the philosophical attitude consists in perceiving an experience *as* a structure.

So, recall your perception of the image above. You perceived this image either as an ugly old hag, or as a young woman. Of course, we are speaking somewhat loosely in putting it this way. You did not perceive the image as an actual person (old hag or young woman), but as a *picture (or drawing)of* one such person. This is obvious enough, but allows us to make an important point, namely that it is also possible to perceive the image above as neither an old hag nor a young woman, but simply as black spots on a page. If you 'perceive the picture as a young woman,' you know that the picture is not a woman. So, whether you perceived the picture as a young woman or an old hag, you clearly also, implicitly, perceived it as black spots on a page (and not an actual person). If you now *strip away* or 'bracket' the interpretation of the picture as an old or young woman, and perceive it as just black spots you have 'reduced' your perception of the image one step closer to a pure state. You see an image of a woman and black spots, then you see black spots, then (if you go all the way) you "'see' the 'seeing' itself in which this givenness, this mode of being, is constituted."[94]

Exercise

1. Return to the image above and try to perceive it not as an old woman or as a young woman, but simply as black spots. Try alternating between the three (old woman, young woman, black spots). Notice that when you change from perceiving it as, say, a young woman to perceiving it as just black spots, you are, in a sense, stripping your young-woman-

---

excellent away to become aware of the expectations with which certain experiences are imbibed, is to ask yourself how you might be surprised by such experiences.
[94]From *The Idea of Phenomenology*, in §22.1 of *Lovers of Wisdom*.

interpretation away from your black-spots-interpretation. Describe anything of interest that you notice as you perform this exercise.

The Phenomenological Reduction of an Intellectual Process

The fact that phenomenological reduction can operate on cognitive processes such as reasoning and calculating, clearly illustrates the difference between this method and rational criticism. Consider the difference between *using* rational criticism to advance our understanding of reality, on the one hand, and *observing* how consciousness behaves when engaging in rational criticism, on the other, and you will see why. For when engaging in rational criticism, one typically takes for granted the cognitive processes involved therein. This is not the case, however, when one engages in phenomenological reduction. Recall Husserl's remark:

> Every intellectual process and indeed every mental process whatever, while being enacted, can be made the object of a pure "seeing" and understanding...

Thus, Husserl does not want to merely engage in intellectual processes such as rational criticism. Rather, Husserl, via phenomenological reduction, wants to *observe* and *analyze what consciousness does* when it engages in intellectual processes like rational criticism.

Let's now try to see how one might start to phenomenologically reduce an intellectual process such as rational criticism. First, we must focus on a specific instance of this activity. We should note that, since we are only focusing on a single instance of rational criticism, it would be misguided to conclude that we are phenomenologically reducing rational criticism *proper*, that is rational criticism in general. Presumably, if one wants to reduce rational criticism proper, one must look at many instances of this activity, and generalize accordingly. With this much understood, let us recall a simple instance of rational criticism from Chapter 2.

An example of rational criticism for phenomenological reduction

Attempt 1: All tables have four legs and a flat surface.

Counterexample 1: No. Some tables have one leg (a single support).

Attempt 2: All tables have one or more legs and a flat surface.

In phenomenological reduction, as you know, one excises theoretical assumptions from the thing being reduced. What are the theoretical assumptions involved in example 2? Since we have presuppositions about tables (we expect them to function in a certain way), flat surfaces (we expect them to have certain properties), and 'legs' (we expect them to support the thing of which they are legs), we must 'bracket' these presuppositions. We must, in a sense, forget about them. Let us do so by substituting the terms 'tables,' 'four legs,' 'flat surface,' 'one leg,' and 'one or more legs' with the letters T, FL, FS, OL, OM, respectively. We can re-present the above instance of rational criticism in the following manner:

Attempt 1: All T have FL and FS.

Counterexample 1: No. Some T have OL.

Attempt 2: All and only T have OM and FS.

Note how after bracketing some of the assumptions involved example 2, it's structure starts to become manifest.

In what sense is the understanding advanced, the 'philosophical attitude' engendered, when we phenomenologically reduce an intellectual process such as rational criticism? Just as we can apprehend an image as a structure, we can likewise apprehend an intellectual process after it is phenomenologically reduced. After phenomenologically reducing example 2, for instance, we can perceive this process *as* a structure in which sentence forms are related in a specific way. As phenomenologically reducing an image reveals the structure of the *world*, phenomenologically reducing an intellectual process, reveals the logical structure of *thinking*, of *cognitive activity*. The philosophical attitude, therefore, empowers the understanding with the ability to apprehend the form, the structure, immanent in every experience.

Before we discuss how Heidegger used phenomenological reduction, let us conclude our discussion of phenomenological reduction by noting that, although both rational criticism and phenomenological reduction can both be used to advance the understanding, they nevertheless comprise different activities. Rational criticism proceeds by *opposing* two theories or statements against each other. In phenomenological reduction, however, there is no movement of opposition. Instead, in phenomenological reduction, one strips, peels, whittles away extraneous assumptions and progresses toward the pure structure implicit in everything. Let us now see how Heidegger used the reductive method in his search for being.

Heidegger

The Reduction of 'Being'

Heidegger criticized Husserl for not using phenomenological reduction on the concept of 'Being.' Husserl, as you now know, wanted to reveal the structure of (i) objects and images, (ii) time, and (iii) intellectual processes. Heidegger asked, what about the fact that these structures exist? What about existence itself? Why isn't phenomenological reduction used to reveal the *structure of existence*? (This does not mean 'the structure of the things that exist,' but the structure of 'existence' itself.) Heidegger proposes his own method, derived from phenomenological reduction, that he uses to reveal the structure of existence. Let us call Heidegger's method 'ontological reduction.' In ontological reduction, one focuses on a specific kind of 'being,' and then brackets from this entity, the presuppositions with which it is associated. This much should sound familiar. But what do we mean by 'specific kind of being?' Intuitively, it seems that Santa Claus, the number 3, rocks, and humans, all subsist in a specific manner. In other words we neither say that 'Santa Claus' exists in the same sense as does the number 3, nor that rocks exist in the same sense as humans. Thus, there are different senses, different modes of existence. In step one of ontological reduction, one must focus on *one* of these modes of existence:

Method	Steps involved
Ontological Reduction	(i) Focus on a specific kind of 'being.'
	(ii) Strip away, 'bracket' from this entity, all theoretical assumptions and presuppositions.

Heidegger, as you have read, focused on the mode of *human* existence or 'Dasein.' For Heidegger believed that Dasein was the sense of being, which, if reduced, revealed the essence, indeed the structure, of existence --the meaning of being. In *Being and Time*, he proceeds to ontologically reduce Dasein, and, as his title suggests, Heidegger understands it's essence as involving a *temporal* structure, as having historicity. Why? because human being is situated in time, because experiences unfold in a sequence of events, and because Dasein cares about how it's time is occupied. Heidegger never completed his ontological reduction of Dasein, and so *Being and Time* remains an incomplete work.

Sartre's Warning

The method of reduction, as we have seen, results in revealing the *essence* of a specific kind of being -- be it image, conception of time, an intellectual process, or Dasein. Although Sartre follows Heidegger in concerning himself with human existence, Sartre warns against thinking of Dasein as having a 'thick' essence. Sartre, in other words, denies that there is such a thing as 'human nature,' or an 'essence of humanity.' This is what is meant by his famous claim, 'existence precedes essence.' What Sartre means by this claim is that, Dasein is neither naturally self-interested, nor naturally virtuous, nor naturally monogamous, and so on. Nevertheless, Sartre does think that Dasein has a 'thin' essence. What is a thin essence? Simply a structure that permits many different possibilities, many different meanings -- an equation that makes use of variables, for instance, or even a blank canvas.

Sartre claims that existence precedes essence, but we can say that it is the *essence* of existence *to precede essence*, and hence that existence does indeed have a *thin* essence. The existence of the canvas precedes the essence of the paining, but the existence of the canvas has an essence -- namely, that it can accompany many possible paintings, many possible essences. Sartre reminds us that human being has a *thin* essence -- like a blank canvas, it can accompany many different possibilities -- hence the diversity of individuals, of cultures, of philosophies, of lives.

A continuity of thought is indeed immanent in the philosophies of Husserl, Heidegger and Sartre. Husserl initiated the initial inquiry into essences, Heidegger reminded us about the essence of being, and Sartre warned against saddling Dasein with an essence that precluded utter freedom. Man is 'condemned to be free' because it is his essence to be so. Sartre suggests that had Heidegger completed his ontological reduction of Dasein, he would have arrived at the barest possible structure -- a skeleton, a temporal frame, devoid of both intrinsic meaning, and intrinsic value. An empty structure.

Chapter 22

The New Metaphysicians

Bradly

1. Describe Bradly form of "absolute idealism".

2. How does Bradly understand the appearance/reality distinction?

Bergson

3. What does Bergson mean when he says that experience will forever be beyond the reach of the intellect?

4. Describe Bergson's philosophical method as demonstrated in his "Introduction to Metaphysics".

5. What on Bergson's view is the essential function of the universe? Why does he think this?

Whitehead

6. What does Whitehead believe about the relation between appearance and reality?

7. What are "actual entities"?

8. What are "eternal objects"?

9. What is the fallacy of misplaced concreteness?

10. What is "ingression"?

11. What was Whitehead's view of physics?

Chapter 23

The Language Philosophers

Frege

What is the nature of linguistic meaning? Someone utters an English sentence and you understand it. This is because you grasp the meaning of the utterance. But what is being grasped? A meaning is not a series of sounds emanating from a speaker's mouth or a string of inkblots on a page. Someone utters the sentence 'Das Buch ist gelb.' If you are like most native English speakers, you do not understand the sentence. Though you do perceive a string of inkblots, you do not grasp its meaning. But what in this case does one fail to grasp? To put it another way, what does the sentence 'The book is yellow' and its German translation, 'Das Buch ist gelb,' have in common? What is it that they share? A meaning, of course! But what is that? Is the meaning of a sentence a physical object? A mental object? Is it an object of some other kind? Or, are meanings not objects at all? What is their nature?

Asking these old questions from a new perspective, Frege set the agenda in the philosophy of language for the twentieth century. Russell, Wittgenstein and Quine were the chief philosophers who carried on and developed the Fregean approach. As you already know, these questions existed before these philosophers asked them, but they were not asked from a philosophy-of-language point of view. Rather, they were asked from the perspective of the philosophy of mind.

The 'Idea' Theory of Meaning

Since John Locke (Chapter 13), many philosophers took the meaning of a word to be the *idea* associated with the word. Frege explains that an idea is a qualitative conscious episode that must have one (and only one) owner. A visual image recalled in memory is an example of such an idea. Call any philosopher who identifies ideas with meanings an *idea theorist*. George Berkeley (Chapter 14) and David Hume (Chapter 15) were also well known idea theorists. When someone says the word 'peach,' you probably call up in your mind a visual image of a peach. That image, an idea theorist would say, is the meaning of the word 'peach.' You understand the utterance, 'peach,' because you grasp an idea of a peach. The reason most English speakers do not understand the word 'Pfirsich,' according to an idea theorist, is that they do not have the correct idea associated with its utterance.

The idea theorists discussed in *Lovers of Wisdom* (Locke, Berkeley and Hume) equate ideas with meanings due to their views about the mind and knowledge. These latter areas of philosophy were of primary concern for them. Frege, of course, brought the philosophy of language to the foreground and showed that many questions of language cannot and should not be framed from the perspective of a philosophy of mind. Before we re-emphasize how Frege did this, we need to understand how the idea theorist accounted for the meanings of whole sentences.

For the idea theorist, the meaning of a sentence is constructed compositionally out of its parts. We understand (know the meaning of) 'the book is yellow' because we have an idea of 'book' and an idea of 'yellow.' Understanding a sentence in which these words occur is a matter of grasping these ideas and somehow putting them together in our heads in the relevant way. So, words in a sentence have ideas associated with them. When these ideas (the meanings of those words) are conjoined, they form a conglomeration of ideas, which idea

114

theorists identify with what we might call 'thoughts.' So, just as sentences are built up out of words, thoughts are built up out of ideas. Such thoughts are the mental entities that, for the idea theorist, are the meanings of sentences.

Frege's Attack on the Idea Theory of Meaning

According to Frege, if the meaning of a word is a mental image associated with the word, then rational discourse (communication, assertion, agreement and disagreement) would be impossible. His argument is fairly simple. Let's go through it step by step.

> (i) If rational discourse (particularly agreement and disagreement) is to be possible, then speakers of the same language must be able to grasp and express the same meanings.

For example, if you argue that cigarettes are not addictive and we disagree, then there is something we are debating. There is a point of contention. It is that cigarettes are addictive. We believe it, you don't. But for us to be having a real disagreement, the point of contention must be the same for the two of us. We must mean the same thing by 'cigarettes are addictive,' otherwise we are not disagreeing, just misunderstanding each other. To exaggerate the point, if you meant by 'cigarettes are addictive' that dishwashing liquid is addictive, and by denying 'cigarettes are addictive' we mean exactly what it is supposed to mean, then we are not having a real disagreement. We are not disagreeing because we are not debating the same thing; we mean different things by 'cigarettes' in this case (the three of us meant cigarettes and you meant dishwashing liquid).

Furthermore,

> (ii) ideas that people associate with the words they use are essentially idiosyncratic.

The images that we associate with the word 'peach' are not identical (maybe not even similar) to the ideas you associate with the word. In fact, we associate with that word a putrid taste that we experienced once when we shared a rotted, worm-infested fruit. You probably do not have this association. And so,

> (iii) If our ideas are the meanings of our words, then speakers of the same language do not grasp and express the same meanings.

But then,

> (iv) rational discourse (including agreement and disagreement) is impossible.

This conclusion follows, since rational discourse requires speakers of a language to share meanings of the words they use.

For Frege, the meaning of a sentence must be something objective, in that it is 'intersubjectively graspable.' That is, more than one speaker of the language must be able to understand it. Why, again, is rational discourse impossible without this sort of objectivity? Frege writes,

> [The idea theorist] would not be able to assert anything at all in the normal sense, and even if his utterances had the form of assertions, they would only have the status of interjections - of expressions of mental states or processes, between which and such

states or processes in another person there could be no contradiction.[95]

According to Frege, a belief or a judgment (the state of acknowledging the truth of a thought) is to be understood on the idea theorist's view as a species of attitude or sensation, like pain or deliciousness. Assertions (the outward manifestations or expressions of judgments) are then to be understood as the manifestations of these sensations. Asserting (in this sense) is the venting of a certain attitude, as wincing is the venting of pain. But as my wincing of pain and your sigh of pleasure do not contradict, neither (on Frege's interpretation of the idea theory of meaning) does our asserting some sentence such as 'cigarettes are addictive' and your denial of it. An apparent disagreement amounts to no more, on this view, than a psychological difference. You think your way, we think our way, and there is no real conflict between our thinking.

An assertion, under such an interpretation, is the manifestation of some brute, contingent attitude, in the way that 'yum' or 'yuk' is the manifestation of the presence of something tasting delicious or disgusting, respectively. A judgment, under such interpretation, is such an attitude or sensation. They reach no further than themselves; they raise no issue of truth or correctness.

Frege considers the venting of an attitude to be a subjective matter. That which ventings express (sensations) are not objective. They are mind-dependent and are not intersubjectively graspable; no one but you has access to them. There is no issue of correctness between our 'yuk' and your 'yum.' We do not disagree in a logically relevant sense. No contradiction exists between 'yuk' and 'yum.' Sensations are also subjective in that sense; they do not contradict. On Frege's view, to confuse asserting with the evincing of attitudes (as the idea theorist must) is to confuse subjectivity for objectivity, to confuse the outward manifestation of inner states and sensations with rational discourse.

The reason why there is no contradiction between 'yuk' and 'yum' is that they are expressions of things that do not stand in logical relations. A sensation is not the kind of thing capable of being true or false. For Frege, linguistic meanings are. They can be in contradiction with each other, because they have truth values and stand in logical relations to one another. When we say, 'Snow is white,' we express something (some linguistic content, or meaning) capable of being true or false. When you say, 'Snow is *not* white,' you disagree; you contradict what we are saying or expressing. Our utterances contradict because they cannot both be true, though they are both truth-evaluable (that is, they are capable of being true or false).

An Experiment

Meanings have a special status. They are truth-evaluable. Frege tells us that no idea theory has the resources to account for this truth-evaluability. Consider the idea you have of 'Napoleon.' Now consider the idea you have of 'dead.' Now put these ideas together. What do you get? You do not get anything capable of being true or false. Do you? Ah, what if we put our idea of 'is' in between our idea of 'Napoleon' and our idea of 'dead.' Do we then get the thought that Napoleon is dead? No, we get three mental do-dads (ideas): one of Napoleon, one of 'is' (whatever that might be), and one of dead.

What seems to be missing is the metaphysical glue that conjoins these ideas in the relevant way so as to create a truth-evaluable entity from our mental images.

Frege argues that such truth-evaluability cannot be accounted for by the idea theorist. From the stacking of ideas one can get a stack of ideas. That's is. No thoughts. A pile of ideas is not enough to account for the constitutive truth-evaluability of thoughts, to account for the special truth-apt status essentially had by the meanings of our sentences. A stack of ideas is not capable of being true or false, it's just a stack of unattached ideas. So much for Frege's criticism of the idea theory of meaning.

---

[95]Frege, "Logic" (1897), in Long and White's translation [1979], p. 133.

Wittgenstein

Wittgenstein was another opponent of the idea theory of meaning. Here is one way he attacked it. He noted that according to an idea theorist a speaker of the language understands a word only if the speaker has the correct idea associated with the word. So speaking the words 'The sky is falling' is not enough to understand the sentence -- one must understand the words, and so, one must have ideas associated with these words. Similarly, if you utter that sentence to someone, they cannot recognize what it is that you are saying unless they recall the appropriate ideas in their head. Without such ideas, according to the idea theorist, they would hear no more than meaningless sounds. Wittgenstein argues that if this sort of idea recollection is required in order to understand someone's utterance, then understanding is impossible altogether. Let us explain.

Wittgenstein's Attack on the Idea Theory

Imagine that all our ideas are (in some sense) stored in an organized way somewhere in our heads (as Locke thought). When a word is uttered, we (very quickly) retrieve the right idea in our minds. Someone says 'rain' and you know what is being referred to. But then someone says 'canard' and you may not know what is being represented, for you may not able to recall the correct idea (if you do not know French). For the idea theorist, correct idea retrieval is understanding (grasping of meaning). Now here's the Wittgensteinian catch. We need to recall an idea of the sky to know the meaning of 'sky.' So we go fishing into our memory banks in search of the right idea. But how do you know that you've found it when you have? How do you know to stop looking when you have stumbled across your sky-idea? According to Wittgenstein, if you knew which idea to retrieve, then you already knew what you were looking for.

So on the idea theory, to understand an utterance, one needs to locate an idea to associate with the utterance. But in order to do that correctly (not arbitrarily), one must have a standard of correctness. In terms of the idea theory, one must have an idea of what they are looking for. Since we are looking for the sky idea, one must have an idea of a sky-idea. But how do we correctly retrieve the standard of correctness (that is, this idea of a sky-idea)? We must have an even further idea of it. But this process goes on to infinity, and surely we do not have an infinite number of ideas in our heads. We are finite beings after all.[96]

An Illustration of Wittgenstein's Criticism

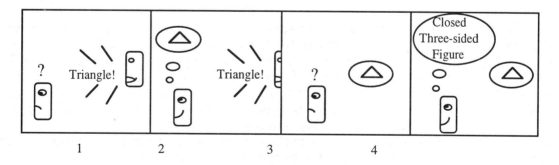

Frame 1: Somebody utters something Until an idea is associated with the sound coming out of this persons mouth, there is only a noise. The listener goes in search of the meaning.

Frame 2: The listener retrieves the correct idea and associates it with the sound uttered. linguistic understanding takes place.

---

[96] This "infinity of ideas" is reminiscent of Parmenides criticism of Plato's theory of forms.

Frame 3: But how did the listener know which idea to retrieve? How did this person know which idea was the triangle-idea?

Frame 4: The listener had an idea of what was being sought. The listener had an idea of a triangle-idea.

Wittgenstein points out that ideas are not even necessary to account for our grasp of meanings. For, if the standard that one uses to pick the right idea of, say, 'triangle' out of one's head good enough to identify the right *idea*, then it must be good enough to identify the *meaning* of 'triangle.' In that case, why does one need to go looking for the idea in the first place? The standard will do just fine.

Wittgenstein argues that recalling occurrent, mental images (ideas) is not at all necessary in order to understand a word. To grasp a word, such as 'triangle', we do not need to call up a mental image of a closed three-sided object in order to associate it with the word. And remember, to assume that we do leads to an infinite regress.

So, if we do not already recognize a conscious mental idea as a triangle-idea, we cannot use it to correctly grasp the word. Wittgenstein's point is that if we do not need an occurrent idea of triangularity to understand the term 'triangle', then the idea theory of meaning is false. If we do need such an idea, as the idea theorist claims, then we need an idea of this idea, and an idea of this idea of an idea, and so, an idea of this idea of an idea of an idea, and so on to infinity. But our minds are finite, therefore the idea theory is false. That is Wittgenstein's criticism of the idea theory of meaning.

Exercises
1.   Both Frege and Wittgenstein attack the idea theory of meaning. Sum up in your own words what they take the problems of the theory to be.

What is Frege's argument against the idea theory of meaning?

What is Wittgenstein's argument against the idea theory of meaning?

Chapter 24

The PostModernists

Gadamer

1. Who was Hermes?

2. What is a system of philosophical hermeneutics?

3. What is the hermeneutic circle? Why does Heidegger believe that the circle is not "vicious"?

4. What is the main thesis of *Truth and Method*?

Merleau-Ponty

5. Expain Merleau-Ponty's criticism of Descartes' *Cogito*.

6. What is a "dialectical" conception of behavior?

7. How, on Merleau-Ponty's view, are the mind and body related? What is his view about mind/body dualism?

Foucault

8. What is "madness" on Foucault's view? And what role does he think it may play in future society?

9. Foucault agrees with Nietzsche's claim that God is dead, but takes it further by adding "So also man, the self, the individual is dead". What does Foucault mean by this? And what is this "self", the death of which he declares?

Derrida

10. What is structuralism?

11. Why does Derrida believe there is no perception?

12. What is deconstruction?